The
Australian
Shepherd

An Owner's Guide To

A HAPPY HEALTHY PET

Howell Book House

Howell Book House
A Simon & Schuster Macmillan Company
1633 Broadway
New York, NY 10019

Library of Congress Cataloging-in-Publication Data
Palika, Liz 1954–
The Australian shepherd: an owner's guide to a happy, healthy pet /Liz Palika
p. cm.

ISBN: 0-87605-503-X

1. Australian Shepherd dog.   I. Title.
SF429.A79P35   1997
636.737—dc21   96-37577
                        CIP

Manufactured in the United States of America
10 9 8 7 6 5 4 3 2

Series Director: Ariel Cannon
Series Assistant Director: Jennifer Liberts
Book Design: Michele Laseau
Cover Design: Iris Jeromnimon
Illustration: Casey Price and Jeff Yesh
Photography:
  Front cover photos: Adult, Toni Tucker; Puppy, Judith Strom
  Back cover photo: Liz Palika
  Joan Balzarini: 27, 62, 96
  Mary Bloom: 96, 136, 145
  Paulette Braun/Pets by Paulette: 18, 41, 45, 50, 61, 67, 91, 96
  Buckinghamhill American Cocker Spaniels: 148
  Sian Cox: 134
  Dr. Ian Dunbar: 98, 101, 103, 111, 116–117, 122, 123, 127
  Ellice Hauta: 9
  Dan Lyons: 96
  Cathy Merrithew: 129
  Liz Palika: 25, 31, 64, 68, 133
  Susan Rezy: 5, 96–97
  Judith Strom: 6, 8, 10, 17, 23, 28, 30, 34, 35, 38-39, 47, 57, 70, 79, 96, 107, 110, 128, 130, 135, 137, 139, 140, 144, 149, 150
  Toni Tucker: 13, 42, 43, 59
  Faith Uridel: 60, 63
  Jean Wentworth: 2-3, 40, 49
  Page 15: courtesy of the Wyoming State Museum
  page 20: Floyd H. McCall, courtesy of Mr. and Mrs. Jay Sisler
Production Team: Kathleen Caulfield, Dave Faust, Trudy Coler and Beth Mayland

Contents

part one

Welcome to the World of the Australian Shepherd

1 What Is an Australian Shepherd? 5

2 The Australian Shepherd's Ancestry 15

3 The World According to the Australian Shepherd 27

part two

Living with an Australian Shepherd

4 Bringing Your Australian Shepherd Home 40

5 Feeding Your Australian Shepherd 49

6 Grooming Your Australian Shepherd 59

7 Keeping Your Australian Shepherd Healthy 67

part three

Enjoying Your Dog

8 Basic Training 98
by Ian Dunbar, Ph.D., MRCVS

9 Getting Active with Your Dog 128
by Bardi McLennan

10 Your Dog and Your Family 136
by Bardi McLennan

11 Your Dog and Your Community 144
by Bardi McLennan

part four

Beyond the Basics

12 Recommended Reading 151

13 Resources 155

Welcome

to the

World

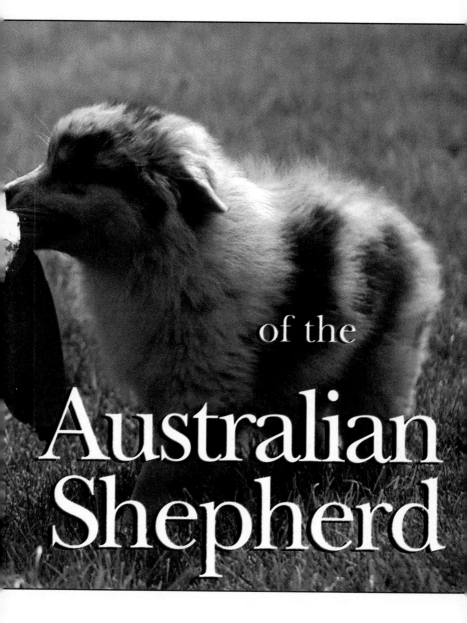

of the

Australian Shepherd

External Features of the Australian Shepherd

- Skull
- Stop
- Muzzle
- Crest
- Neck
- Withers
- Back
- Shoulder
- Stifle or Knee
- Toes
- Hock

chapter 1

What
Is an
Australian
Shepherd?

Introduction to the Standard

What is a standard? Each breed of dog recognized by a dog registry, such as the Australian Shepherd Club of America or the American Kennel Club (AKC), has a written description called the "standard." The standard is a verbal picture of the ideal dog of that breed, describing every aspect of its appearance and demeanor in detail. It is written by people with expert knowledge of the

breed, usually a club or committee composed of long-time breeders, exhibitors and judges.

When a dog competes in a dog show, he is judged not only against the other dogs of his breed competing that day, but also against the written standard. The dog who wins is the dog who most closely fits the written description, compared to the other dogs competing. The standard is also used to choose dogs for breeding. Breeders use the standard as a guideline to determine which dogs or bitches should pass on their genes to future generations.

Excerpts from the Australian Shepherd standards, as approved by the Australian Shepherd Club of America (ASCA) in 1977 and the American Kennel Club (AKC) in 1993, are given in the following pages with comments. There are two standards for the Australian Shepherd. The American Kennel Club's standards differ somewhat from the original standards of the ASCA. However, both describe a medium sized working dog and an active, loyal companion.

General Appearance

(ASCA) *The Australian Shepherd is a well-balanced dog of medium size and bone. He is attentive and animated, showing strength and stamina combined with unusual agility. Slightly longer than tall, he has a coat of moderate length and*

coarseness with coloring that offers variety and individuality in each specimen. An identifying characteristic is his natural or docked bobtail. In each sex, masculinity or femininity is well-defined.

(AKC) *The Australian Shepherd is an intelligent working dog with strong herding and guarding instincts. He is a loyal companion and has the stamina to work all day. He is well-balanced, slightly longer than tall and of medium size and bone, with color that offers variety and individuality. He is attentive and animated, lithe and agile, solid and muscular without cloddiness. He has a coat of moderate length and coarseness. He has a docked or natural bobbed tail.*

The Australian Shepherd has an alert, intelligent expression.

These introductory paragraphs set the stage for the rest of the standard. They both describe a well-proportioned dog of medium size capable of working hard—an athlete. Both standards mention individuality as a trait of the breed; all Aussies are not meant to look the same, though they do have fundamental traits in common. This variety and large gene pool keeps the breed vigorous and healthy. The ASCA description specifically mentions the difference between males and females. The AKC addresses sex distinctions in later paragraphs.

Character and Temperament

(ASCA) *The Australian Shepherd is intelligent, and is primarily a working dog of strong herding and guardian in-stincts. He is an exceptional companion. He is versatile and easily trained, performing his assigned tasks with great style and enthusiasm. He is reserved with strangers but does not exhibit shyness. Although he is an aggressive, authoritative worker, viciousness toward people or animals is intolerable.*

(AKC) *The Australian Shepherd is an intelligent, active dog with an even disposition; he is good-natured and is seldom quarrelsome. He may be somewhat reserved in initial meetings. Faults: Any display of shyness, fear or aggression is to be severely penalized.*

Both standards mention that the dog should not be shy, fearful or aggressive toward people. An Australian Shepherd with the correct character or temperament is a dog willing to work for his owner, a dog to be treasured for his loyalty, intelligence and versatility.

Head

(ASCA) *Clean-cut, strong, dry and in proportion to the body. The top-skull is flat to slightly rounded, its length and width each equal to the length of the muzzle which is in balance and proportioned to the rest of the head. The muzzle tapers slightly to a rounded tip. The stop is moderate but well-defined.*

(AKC) *The head is clean-cut, strong and dry. Overall size should be in proportion to the body. The muzzle is equal in* *length or slightly shorter than the back skull. Viewed from the side, the topline of the back-skull and muzzle form parallel planes, divided by a moderate, well-defined stop. The muzzle tapers little from base to nose and is rounded at the tip.*

There are two slightly different pictures here. ASCA wants a top-skull "flat to slightly rounded," not dome shaped. The AKC prefers to see the "topline of the back-skull and muzzle form parallel planes," which is evidently flatter than the ASCA's "slightly rounded" version.

EXPRESSION

(AKC) *Showing attentiveness and intelligence, alert and eager. Gaze should be keen but friendly.*

EYES

(ASCA) *Very expressive, showing attentiveness and intelligence. Clear, almond-shaped, and of moderate size, set a little obliquely, neither prominent or sunken, with pupils dark, well-defined and perfectly positioned. Color is brown, blue, amber or any variation or combination, including flecks and marbling.*

Your Australian Shepherd will probably not fit all the requirements of the standard, but he will still be a loyal friend and companion.

(AKC) *Eyes are brown, blue, amber or any variation or combination thereof, including flecks or marbling. Almond-shaped, not protruding nor sunken. The blue merles and blacks have black pigmentation on eye rims. The reds and red merles have liver (brown) pigmentation on eye rims.*

Eye color in the Australian Shepherd is an outstanding feature of the breed. An individual Aussie may have different colored eyes; a single iris may even have different colors in it. These striking eyes give the dog a focused, intelligent expression.

A notable difference between the two paragraphs addressing eyes is the mention of the oblique eye set in the ASCA standard. An oblique eye set is said to be dependent upon the zygomatic arch. The flatter the arch, the more oblique the eye set. When the curve of the arch is more prominent, the eyes will be set more toward the front of the head. The moderate arch called for in the ASCA standard is enough arch for good front and side vision but flat enough for protection from the dangers associated with the breed's natural work: bushes, brambles and the debris thrown up by flying hooves.

The ASCA standard also calls for perfectly positioned pupils. Unfortunately, the breed has been known to have some eye defects, and an off-set pupil is an easily seen defect that may be a clue to underlying problems.

TEETH

(ASCA) *A full complement of strong, white teeth meet in a scissors bite. An even bite is a fault. Teeth broken or missing by accident are not to be penalized. Disqualifications: Undershot bites, overshot exceeding ¹/₈ inch.*

(AKC) *A full complement of strong, white teeth should meet in a scissors bite or may meet in a level bite. Disqualifications: Undershot, overshot by greater than 1/8 inch. Loss of contact caused by short center incisors in an otherwise correct bite shall not be judged undershot. Teeth missing or broken by accident shall not be penalized.*

When the AKC standard was adopted, many people were concerned with the acceptance of a level or even bite. Most canine bite experts feel a scissors bite is indicative of a proper jaw assembly and the scissors bite allows a herding dog to properly "grip" livestock with a pinching motion instead of a puncturing bite. Other experts feel that teeth in an even jaw are more prone to wear

Aussies' eyes are an outstanding feature of the breed, and can be multi-colored, marbled or flecked.

by the constant meeting of teeth and are more apt to be injured or broken.

EARS

(ASCA) *Set high at the side of the head, triangular and slightly rounded at the tip, of moderate size with the length measured by bringing the tip of the ear around to the inside corner of the eye. The ears, at full attention, break slightly forward and over from one-quarter to one-half above the base. Prick ears and hound type ears are severe faults.*

(AKC) *Ears are triangular of moderate size and leather, set high at the head. At full attention they break forward and over, or to the side as a rose ear. Prick ears and hanging ears are severe faults.*

The Aussie's herding heritage has produced a strong, athletic working dog.

Neck and Body

(ASCA) *The neck is firm, clean and in proportion to the body. It is of medium length and slightly arched at the crest, setting well into the shoulders. The body is firm and muscular. The topline appears level at a natural four-square stance. The chest is deep and strong with ribs well-sprung. The loin is strong and broad when viewed from the top. The bottom line carries well back with a moderate tuck-up. The croup is moderately sloping, the ideal being thirty (30) degrees from the horizontal. The tail is straight, not to exceed four (4) inches, natural bobtail or docked.*

(AKC) *Neck is strong, of moderate length slightly arched at the crest, fitting well into the shoulders.*

Topline. Back is straight and strong, level and firm from withers to hip joints. The croup is moderately sloped.

Chest is not broad but is deep with the lowest point reaching the elbow. The ribs are well-sprung and long, neither barrel chested nor slab sided. The underline shows a moderate tuck-up.

Tail is straight, docked or naturally bobbed, not to exceed four inches in length.

The neck and body sections of both standards describe a fit, strong dog who is versatile and able to work hard and efficiently.

Color

(ASCA) *All colors are strong, clear and rich. The recognized colors are blue merle, red (liver) merle, solid black and solid red (liver) all with or without white marking and/or tan (copper) points with no reference. The blue merle and black have black pigmentation of the nose, lips and eye rims; the red (liver) and red (liver) merle have liver pigmentation on nose, lips and eye rims. Butterfly nose should not be faulted under one year of age. On all colors, the areas surrounding the ears and eyes are dominated by color other than white. The hairline of the white collar does not ex-ceed the point of the withers. Disqualifi-cations: Other than recognized colors. White body splashes. Dudley nose.*

(AKC) *Blue merle, black, red merle, red—all with or without white marking and/or tan (copper) points, with no order of preference. The hairline of a white collar does not exceed the*

> **THE AMERICAN KENNEL CLUB**
>
> Familiarly referred to as "the AKC," the American Kennel Club is a nonprofit organization devoted to the advancement of purebred dogs. The AKC maintains a registry of recognized breeds and adopts and enforces rules for dog events including shows, obedience trials, field trials, hunting tests, lure coursing, herding, earthdog trials, agility and the Canine Good Citizen program. It is a club of clubs, established in 1884 and composed, today, of over 500 autonomous dog clubs throughout the United States. Each club is represented by a delegate; the delegates make up the legislative body of the AKC, voting on rules and electing directors. The American Kennel Club maintains the Stud Book, the record of every dog ever registered with the AKC, and publishes a variety of materials on purebred dogs, including a monthly magazine, books and numerous educational pamphlets. For more information, contact the AKC at the address listed in Chapter 13, "Resources," and look for the names of their publications in Chapter 12, "Recommended Reading."

point of the withers at the skin. White is acceptable on the neck (either in part or as a full collar) chest, legs, muzzle, underparts, blaze on head and white extension up to four inches measuring from a horizontal line at the elbow. White on the head should not predominate and the eyes must be fully surrounded by color and pigment. Merles characteristically become darker with increasing age. Disqualifications: White body splashes.

The ASCA standard mentions "rich" colors, and this truly describes the striking color combinations of the Aussie. The colors of the Australian Shepherd are very important to the identity of the breed and are part of what makes this such a beautiful, unique breed.

WHAT IS A BREED STANDARD?

A breed standard—a detailed description of an individual breed—is meant to portray the *ideal* specimen of that breed. This includes ideal structure, temperament, gait, type—all aspects of the dog. Because the standard describes an ideal specimen, it isn't based on any particular dog. It is a concept against which judges compare actual dogs and breeders strive to produce dogs. At a dog show, the dog that wins is the one that comes closest, in the judge's opinion, to the standard for its breed. Breed standards are written by the breed parent clubs, the national organizations formed to oversee the well-being of the breed. They are voted on and approved by the members of the parent clubs.

Gait

(ASCA) *Smooth, free and easy; exhibiting agility of movement with a well-balanced, ground-covering stride. Fore and rear legs move straight and parallel with the center line of the body; as speed increases, the feet, both front and rear, converge toward the center line of gravity of the dog, while the topline remains firm and level.*

(AKC) *The Australian Shepherd has a smooth, free and easy gait. He exhibits great agility of movement with a well-balanced, ground covering stride. Fore and hind legs move straight and parallel with the center line of the body. As speed increases, the feet, front and rear, converge towards the center line of gravity of the dog while the back remains firm and level. The Australian Shepherd must be agile and able to change direction or gait instantly.*

The Australian Shepherd is, first and foremost, an athlete. The breed's heritage as an active herding dog required this. Today, as a breed active in many dog sports, including obedience, agility and flyball, a natural athleticism is needed.

Size

(ASCA) *Preferred height at the withers for males is 20–23 inches; that for females is 18–21 inches, however, quality is not to be sacrificed in favor of size.*

(AKC) *The preferred height for males is 20–23 inches and females 18–21 inches. Quality is not to be sacrificed in favor of size.*

PROPORTION

(AKC) *Measuring from breastbone to the rear of the thigh and from the top of the withers to the ground, the Australian Shepherd is slightly longer than tall.*

SUBSTANCE

(AKC) *Solidly built with moderate bone. Structure in males reflects masculinity without coarseness. Bitches appear feminine without being slight of bone.*

Understanding What the Words Mean

If you're having trouble picturing in your mind what these words actually mean, try reading the standard with your Australian Shepherd standing in front of you. Compare the words to your dog. Do you see what they are describing?

If you still have questions, go to a dog show and find people with Australian Shepherds. Ask a couple of different people how they interpret the standard, or portions of the standard, and ask them to demonstrate on a dog. Also, after the judging is completed, many judges will be happy to express an opinion about the standard and dogs in general.

Australian Shepherds come in many different and beautiful color combinations. Pictured here is a red merle.

13

Australian Shepherds clubs often host seminars, where judges and breeders speak on a variety of subjects, including the breed standard. Ask your local club if anything is planned for the future.

The different viewpoints expressed by a variety of people will either clarify the standard for you—or totally confuse you. Just keep in mind that the standard is made up of words, and words have different meanings to different people, so there will always be some differences in opinion. Also, applying the descriptions, no matter how well they are written, to living, breathing dogs can be very difficult.

chapter 2

The
Australian
Shepherd's
Ancestry

Most researchers think that dogs have been a part of mankind's history for at least 12,000 years. Cave drawings, gravesites and other archeological evidence support this time frame. What researchers don't agree on is exactly what the first dogs might have been like. Were they wolves or the early ancestors of wolves? The first canine companion may have been a hun-

Wyoming, circa 1900

gry, injured or otherwise incapacitated wolf drawn to a cave by meat scraps, or it might have been an orphaned cub raised by a child or a lonely hunter. We can only imagine the circumstances that led to this first connection between humans and canines.

Herding Heritage

The first occupation for dogs was guarding the family or tribe's cave, warning of predators and trespassers. Dogs most certainly helped on the hunt for food, and as mankind domesticated other animals, dogs were used to protect and care for the family's livestock. Humans began to depend more and more on livestock and less on hunting, and protection of herds was necessary to ensure a family's livelihood and sustenance. Herding dogs became critical to mankind's survival.

Herding dogs were bred to work in numerous terrains and climates with a variety of livestock, including sheep, goats, cattle and ducks. Over thousands of years, herding dogs of various types were developed all over the world. There were long-coated, corded Pulis in Hungary; silky-coated Border Collies in Great Britain; massive Bouvier des Flandres in Belgium and a variety of other breeds of all sizes, shapes, temperaments and coat types.

It is from this mix of herding breeds that the Australian Shepherd most likely evolved, but the breed's early history is unknown. Some breed historians feel that the Aussie is a mixture of herding breeds that came to America with early settlers from Europe. Other researchers are convinced that the breed originated in Europe, went to Australia and then came to California and North America during the Gold Rush. The myths that surround the origins of the breed are one of its tantalizing

WHERE DID DOGS COME FROM?

It can be argued that dogs were right there at man's side from the beginning of time. As soon as human beings began to document their existence, the dog was among their drawings and inscriptions. Dogs were not just friends, they served a purpose: There were dogs to hunt birds, pull sleds, herd sheep, burrow after rats—even sit in laps! What your dog was originally bred to do influences the way it behaves. The American Kennel Club recognizes over 140 breeds, and there are hundreds more distinct breeds around the world. To make sense of the breeds, they are grouped according to their size or function. The AKC has seven groups:

1) Sporting, 2) Working,
3) Herding, 4) Hounds,
5) Terriers, 6) Toys,
7) Nonsporting

Can you name a breed from each group? Here's some help: (1) Golden Retriever; (2) Doberman Pinscher; (3) Collie; (4) Beagle; (5) Scottish Terrier; (6) Maltese; and (7) Dalmatian. All modern domestic dogs (Canis familiaris) are related, however different they look, and are all descended from Canis lupus, the gray wolf.

aspects. Below, we'll briefly explore the possible origins of the Aussie. Take a moment to think about it for yourself and decide what makes the most sense to you.

Herding Dogs in the New World

Early American history is threaded with bits of information concerning sheep, shepherds and their herding dogs. Christopher Columbus, who made four trips to the New World (1492-1502), brought sheep with him to North America on at least two of his trips. The British explorers (early 1600's) did not bring sheep with them that we know of, but the settlers who followed them did, and with these sheep came their dogs. The British herding dogs included Dorset Blue Shags, Smithfield Sheepdogs and Cumberland Sheepdogs. The Blue Shag and the Smithfield are related to the old Scottish Collie and the Cumberland is a Border Collie-type dog.

Herding dogs have been valued as workers and companions for centuries.

The Spanish also figured prominently among settlers who brought domestic animals to the New World. Merino sheep and their wonderful wool had ensured Spain a primary place in the world trade markets in the 1500s and 1600s, and sheep were the mainstay of the economy. When Spanish immigrants came to the Americas, both North and South, they brought their sheep.

By the late 1600s and early 1700s, immigrants from several nations were flooding into North America, some bringing the tools of their trade, others just the shirts on their backs. People who worked the land in their native countries knew the importance of livestock and brought their livestock and dogs with them to the New World. Immigrants from Scotland brought the Scottish Collie (a Bearded Collie-type dog) with them;

17

immigrants from Wales brought along the Welsh Grey Sheepdog, also a Bearded Collie-type dog. The French imported the Bouvier des Flandres and the Germans, who also brought Merino sheep to the New World, brought along their German Shepherds and the Hutespitz, a Spitz-type dog.

The history of the Australian Shepherd is bound up with tales of the American West.

One of the popular herding dogs imported was the English Shepherd. Called a farm collie or ranch collie in early America, the English Shepherd could herd livestock, protect the family against wild animals and warn off trespassers. The English Shepherd today looks much like an Australian Shepherd with a tail. This similarity suggests to many that the English Shepherd is an ancestor of today's Australian Shep-herd, though there is no definitive way to prove it.

As immigrants and their dogs settled in America from all over Europe, crossings of the various breeds took place. Eventually, as the different regions were settled and communities were established, each area developed a particular type of herding dog suited to their particular needs. These dogs were called by a variety of names, including Spanish Shepherd, Bobtails, California Shepherds, Pastor dogs and New Mexico Shepherds.

The Australian Shepherd in the American West

The California Gold Rush brought a flood of people to California. Some sought to make their fortunes panning for gold, while others made a fortune selling equipment to the miners, often at outrageous prices. Food was sometimes in short supply, and flocks of sheep were brought in to feed and clothe the hordes.

The history of the West during the late 1800s is filled with tall tales, and the Australian Shepherd's history during this time period is no exception. Leaving the romance of the Wild West aside, most of the people who moved westward in the 1800s had modest dreams of starting a new life, buying land where they could farm and raise a family. Other than a few personal diaries, written records from the early years are almost nonexistent. A few photographs do remain that show dogs resembling the Australian Shepherd posing with Western homesteaders and their families. A loyal, trainable herding dog was needed and the Aussie, as the breed type was beginning to be known, fit right in.

Stories abound as to how the breed became known as the "Australian Shepherd." Notes in personal diaries, stories told to grandchildren and old photographs show us that a dog very similar to today's Aussie was an integral part of early North American, and especially Western, life.

But where did it come from? It might be a cross-breeding of British-type herding dogs that served as farm dogs all over the country or it might have come from the Basque country of Europe by way of Australia. Or it might be a combination of all of the above. Like many Americans, the Aussie is very much a part of the American melting pot. Although the breed is and has been known as the Australian Shepherd, it is very much an American breed.

The Aussie in Australia

In the 1700s, people were immigrating to Australia as well as to North America. The Germans, French, Irish,

Welsh and English moved there, bringing their live-stock and dogs. The German Coulie is a herding dog that looks much like today's Aussie and might figure in the breed's heritage. The British immigrated in large numbers, infusing Australia with their customs, language and of course, their dogs.

As the popularity of sheep herding spread throughout Australia, herding dogs became a necessity. When Merino sheep were imported, Spanish and Basque shepherds came to care for them, bringing their Pyrenees sheepdogs and Catalan sheepdogs. As in North America, a lot of mixed breeding took place, some intentional, some by accident.

The Basque Factor

The Basque people live in the western Pyrenees in France and Spain. The Basque language has no known relationship to any other language in the world and it does not have a written form; history is passed on through stories and songs told over generations.

Jay Sisler and his talented Aussies are shown here performing at the National Western Stockdog Show in 1954. Their talented feats won audiences over to this new breed.

The Basque people are credited with the development of some wonderful herding dogs, including, some say, the ancestors of the Australian Shepherd. Many Aussie historians believe that the modern Aussie is the descendant of Basque sheepdogs that went to Australia

and then to North America, following the herds
of sheep. The Basque people did have some nice
herding dogs that were eagerly sought after by other
shepherds, and there are reports of dogs being
imported from Spain in the 1800s. As with many of the
herding dogs imported to Australia and North
America, these dogs were often crossed with other
herding dogs; breed integrity was not important, a
good working dog was.

However, one fact that many historians either do not
realize or have forgotten is that many Basque immigrants to both Australia and North America were not
shepherds in their homelands. Some were, of course,
but many of the Basque immigrants came to America
for the same reasons that immigrants from other countries came: to make a living or a fortune, to have more
personal freedom or simply to better themselves.
When they found that the streets were not paved with
gold, they applied their work ethic and drive to suc-
ceed to learning from local shepherds how to care for
livestock. Though the Basque people may have been
great shepherds, it is quite possible that they did not
bring their dogs with them in significant numbers.

The Aussie Becomes Established

Over the years, a breed type began to emerge. People
appreciated the intelligence, trainability, and athleticism of the Aussies, and they tried to breed similar
dogs together to retain these treasured traits. In the
western United States, some dedicated fans of the
breed began to popularize the Aussie by spreading
the word about this talented breed.

"BLUE DOGS"

Jay Sisler, a talented dog trainer from Idaho, had
Aussies before the breed was well-known as the
Australian Shepherd. He acquired Keno, his first "blue
dog," as he called them, in 1939. He did more to pro-
mote the Australian Shepherd than anyone else in the

breed's history. Sisler spent twenty years of his life traveling with his "blue dogs," giving shows at rodeos and amazing people with the tricks that his wonderfully trained dogs could do.

His foundation bitch, Blue Star, was bought at a livestock auction. Her pedigree is unknown, but when bred to Keno, she produced Shorty and Stub. These two dogs went on to be two of Sisler's most impressive rodeo trick dogs.

Sisler and his dogs performed in the 1950s and 1960s. Crowds everywhere agreed that his dogs were absolutely amazing. They would stand on their heads, balance on bars, jump rope, climb ladders and much, much more. Their acts greatly increased interest in the breed, especially in the Northwestern United States and Canada.

Sisler was not a breeder as many people define it; he did not breed a great number of litters. However, he and his brother Gene did breed a few dogs that contributed to many of the modern Aussie lines, passing on intelligence, trainability and a desire to work.

Sisler's Shorty (1948-1959) sired many of the breed's most important foundation stock. He was a good looking, great working blue merle with lots of personality. He was the star of Sisler's act for a number of years and a Walt Disney movie, *Cowdog* was based on his life and talents. Today, his lines show up in many modern pedigrees.

FLINTRIDGE

Noel Heard acquired a red herding dog named Old Jim in 1928. Old Jim was said to be an Australian Shepherd, out of a blue merle bitch. After growing up with Old Jim, Noel's son, Weldon, a veterinarian schooled in genetics, recommended a client to an Aussie breeder, Fletcher Wood, and through a convoluted chain of events, ended up with an Aussie bitch named Mistingo. Mistingo was bred to Harper's Old Smokey, one of the breed's foundation sires, producing two pups, one of which was Heard's Blue Spice of

Flintridge, who became Dr. Heard's foundation bitch. She was bred back to Old Smokey, producing Heard's Salt of Flintridge and Heard's Chili of Flintridge, both of whom produced a number of champions in the 1970s and are still seen on pedigrees today.

Dr Heard's biggest contribution to the breed was his practice of strong linebreeding with good quality dogs, defining quality as a combination of conformation, working ability and intelligence. This standardized his line, creating dogs of close type and quality.

Today , Aussies excel in many dog sports; this one is clearing a hoop in obedience.

STEVE MANSKER

Steve Mansker saw Jay Sisler and his dogs at numerous rodeos in the late 1940s and decided that he wanted one of those dogs. He bought Sisler's Freckles in 1956. Freckles was bred to Green's Kim, a large blue merle who was an outstanding cowdog. Mansker's dogs were talented workers, as well as attractive and intelligent animals. Mansker used judicious linebreeding to keep the great working instinct that he had in his early dogs. These dogs went on to establish the foundation of many of today's important working kennels.

The Aussie Today

The versatility of the Australian Shepherd is remarkable. Today's Australian Shepherd is an active and intelligent companion who requires stimulation and

23

activity. There are very few breeds of dogs capable of performing as many different jobs as the Australian Shepherd. The breed's easy trainability, intelligence, common sense and problem solving abilities, combined with a medium size build, an easy-to-care-for coat, a strong will to work and incredible loyalty make for a great working and playing companion.

In 1991, the Australian Shepherd was admitted into the American Kennel Club. Some feared this would mean the breed's deterioration into an attractive show dog with little working ability. After several attempts, however, admission into the AKC was final. The Australian Shepherd can now participate in any activity sponsored by the AKC, including obedience, agility and tracking competitions. Many AKC activities are mentioned below; also see Chapter 9, "Getting Active with Your Dog," for more information about activities you and your Aussie can do together.

STOCKDOG

As we have seen, the breed's first occupation was as a stockdog. Aussies are able to work a variety of livestock in different situations and terrain. They can be soft enough to work ewes and lambs and tough enough to handle range cattle. Aussies can drive, move and gather livestock on the range, in a small farm setting, or in stockdog trials.

SEARCH AND RESCUE

The Aussie's strong work ethic, intelligence and good scenting abilities have made it a premier search and rescue dog. Trained dogs and their owners have found lost hikers, children who have wandered away, and elderly people who have become confused and lost. Search and rescue trained Aussies have worked to find flood victims and people swept away by mudslides and avalanches. Although St. Bernards are the most famous search and rescue dogs, and German Shepherd Dogs are the most commonly seen search dogs, Aussies are rapidly becoming the breed of choice for many search and rescue people.

TRACKING

Tracking is an activity that allows the dog to use its naturally acute sense of smell. Tracking can be a competitive sport in which prizes and titles are awarded; it can be a recreational activity ("Go find Dad! Where is he?") or it can be part of a search and rescue effort. Again, the Aussie's trainability, work ethic, intelligence and natural abilities make tracking something that Aussies can, and do, excel in.

SERVICE DOGS

Service dogs work to provide personal assistance to their physically challenged owners. These dogs might retrieve dropped items, open doors, get items out of the refrigerator, or pull wheelchairs. Hearing alert dogs notify their owner to noises in the environment, including smoke detectors and a baby's crying. Service dogs provide their owners with aid, independence, and an important social icebreaker. After all, everyone wants to talk about a working dog.

As a therapy dog, an Aussie can offer irreplaceable affection and attention to those who need it most.

Aussies have been used more and more as service dogs in the last few years. Robert Krause was injured in a diving accident and now lives a much fuller life because of an Australian Shepherd. His canine partner, Kimba, retrieves household items identified by name, pulls his wheelchair and gives him ample love and affection. Kimba has even protected Robert from a would-be burglar. Robert says that Kimba is, without question, his best friend.

GUIDE DOGS

Most guide dogs are larger breeds, such as German Shepherd dogs or Labrador Retrievers. However, a larger dog can also cause larger problems. Several guide dog schools started using the Australian Shepherd several years ago and have found the breed to be very good at this work. When partnered with teenagers, women or smaller men, the breed has been up to the challenge, and in fact, worked out better than anyone (except of course, an Aussie fan!) expected.

THERAPY DOGS

Therapy dogs go with their owners to nursing homes, schools, day care centers, and hospitals and share love and affection with people who need it. Many people assume that because Aussies are supposed to be reserved with strangers and protective of their people, the breed cannot work as a therapy dog, but nothing is further from the truth. If an Australian Shepherd is well socialized to many different people as a puppy and young dog, it will quickly learn what is expected during therapy dog work.

My young Aussie, Dax, comes from strong working stockdog lines and is an energetic, protective, strong-willed dog. She is very cautious of strangers and is quick to alert me to trespassers. However, when I put her therapy bandanna on her and we pull up in front of the nursing home, she changes. She becomes quieter, gentler and more affectionate. She noses a person's hand until he/she rests it on her head and then she sits still as the person strokes her. She allows handling and even rough treatment that she wouldn't tolerate in any other situation.

OTHER ACTIVITIES

Aussies are great competitive obedience dogs (as long as their owners are smart enough to teach them!). They have competed in Frisbee competitions and have won several World Frisbee Championships. Australian Shepherds have pulled sleds and skiers. In fact, there is a competitive team of racing sled dogs made up entirely of Aussies! Aussies play flyball, excel in agility, pull wagons, go hiking and much, much more.

chapter 3

The **World**
According to the
Australian
Shepherd

Above All, A Herding Dog

The Australian Shepherd is, first and foremost, a herding dog. Although many Aussies are involved in other activities and dog sports, the breed's herding heritage is still strong, even in those Aussies who have never seen a sheep. Sasha, a blue merle Aussie who was raised in the city,

had never seen any livestock until her owner took her to a herding instinct test when she was four years old. Her lack of exposure didn't seem to matter at all. Sasha watched the sheep for a few seconds, dashed out and around them, gathered them up and brought them to her owner.

A Herding Dog as a Pet

Herding instincts, chase instincts and prey drive are closely related. In fact, an overenthusiastic or unsupervised herding dog of any breed can become a stock killer. This prey drive or chase instinct can cause a dog to chase anything that moves: sheep, cattle, cats, cars or children. Naturally, this can be a good talent when developed properly in a working herding dog, but it can cause problems when the dog chases cars or children or kills livestock.

Aussies with Children

Aussies will be loyal family members and active, energetic companions for young children. As with any dog, you are responsible for making sure dog and child interact peacefully. Your Aussie must be trained to respect even the little people in his life, and your children must learn how to treat their dog properly.

Aussies are loyal protectors and companions to the family's children.

Children need to know that a dog is not a plaything, and that he shouldn't be treated as such. Ear-pulling, tail-grabbing and teasing will try the patience of even the most even-tempered dog. Older children who have been taught properly can be excellent with dogs. If you are unsure about the situation, supervise their interactions until you are secure.

Herding dogs can show their talents in a variety of ways, one of which is by nipping at family member's heels as they would do to get cattle moving. Obviously, this is undesirable in a family or companion dog. Another herding instinct is circling. With sheep or cattle, the dog runs a circle or boundary around the herd or flock to keep the animals together. Again, this is great in a working dog but can be extremely annoying when the dog won't let the kids leave a ten foot circle he has arbitrarily set up as a boundary.

Although herding instincts are very strong, they can be controlled by teaching the dog what is allowed and what isn't and by allowing the dog to use its instincts constructively. If the kids get angry when the dog keeps them herded into a small circle, teach the dog what the real boundaries are. On the other hand, the Aussie's herding instincts may be just the thing in some situations: many a toddler has been prevented from wandering away by an alert Aussie.

PROTECTIVE INSTINCTS

The Australian Shepherd's instincts to guard his property come from his herding instincts, too. The herding dog is often also required to alert the shepherd to the presence of predators, trespassers or thieves. When there is no flock to protect, the Aussie protects his people instead. This protective instinct can be seen every day: in the dog's active barking when someone approaches the house, and in the dog's low growl when a stranger approaches the family children.

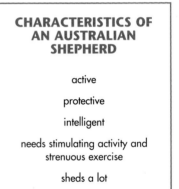

CHARACTERISTICS OF AN AUSTRALIAN SHEPHERD

active

protective

intelligent

needs stimulating activity and strenuous exercise

sheds a lot

This protective instinct, combined with the breed's herding instincts and desire to work, is what makes the breed so valuable to people who need a working dog.

A RESERVED JUDGE

These instincts also cause many people to view the breed as stand-offish or reserved, as well they should. The Australian Shepherd will not greet every person as a friend. The Aussie is not one to go about with a wiggling behind and a licking tongue; other dogs can do that. Instead, the Aussie will watch people approach and look them in the eye. Some people have said that this stare is "taking a person's measure." If you pass this scrutiny, you will be greeted with reserve. If you do not pass the measure, you will be greeted with a growl.

This doesn't mean Aussies are cold or unfeeling. Known friends are greeted with enthusiasm, a wiggling behind, a dancing body, a licking tongue and verbal chatter, even barking. Aussies have a great memory and will remember friends, even ones they haven't seen in years.

A STRONG DRIVE TO WORK

All Australian Shepherds need to have a job. Because the breed was derived from herding dogs and was designed to work, Aussies need an occupation, something to keep the mind challenged and the body busy.

A bored Aussie will become a bad Aussie, guaranteed. Many bored Aussies dig up the back yard, uproot plants, chew on the lawn furniture, bark incessantly and try to escape from the yard.

There are quite a few different jobs that you can give your dog. Use obedience training to give him some structure in his life. This can teach him to work for you and to listen to your commands. Teach him to bring in the morning newspaper and to find your slippers and your keys. Teach him to find family members by name. Find someone in your area who gives herding lessons and enroll in a class. Find a dog training club in your area that can teach both of you something new, like agility, flyball or scent hurdle races. Teach your dog to play Frisbee. All of these things will keep your Aussie busy, focused and happy.

An Aussie will define and protect his boundaries eagerly.

Living With an Australian Shepherd

The Australian Shepherd is a medium sized dog, averaging between forty-five to sixty pounds. That means a forty-five to sixty pound dog curled up by your side on the sofa or stretched out across your feet. Although an Australian Shepherd is not a large dog, his heart is. Everything an Aussie does, he does in a big way. When an Aussie loves you, he loves you totally and unconditionally. When a working Aussie guides his blind owner, works for a rancher, accepts obedience training, searches for a lost person, or even sleeps on your sofa, he does so thoroughly, totally and completely. If you have an Aussie, you will always have a dog as a shadow; you will never, ever be alone again. The easiest way to torture an Aussie is to lock him outside or separate him from his people.

Aussies are affectionate and loyal to those they consider friends.

A POWERFUL DOG

The Australian Shepherd is an amazingly strong dog for its size; both in physical strength and in stamina. Aussies love to play athletic games, such as Frisbee, in which they can use their strength, stamina and athletic prowess. Because of his strength, an Aussie without training could easily jump up and knock down a child, a senior citizen or even an unprepared adult. With training, Aussies can learn to control their power, using it only when required.

ACUTE SENSES

As with most dogs, the senses of smell and hearing are the most important senses to the Australian Shepherd. Unlike many other breeds, the sense of sight is also

very important. Touch and taste are also used, but not
to the extremes that hearing, smell and sight are.

The Aussie's sense of smell is so acute that we can
barely comprehend it. Dogs taught to use their sense
of smell as an occupation, such as narcotic detection
dogs, can distinguish between two 20 gallon tubs of
water, one of which has a teaspoon of salt dissolved in
it. Considering that we find salt to be odorless, this ability is amazing. Because their sense of smell is so acute,
many Aussies spend quite a bit of time smelling the
grass, sniffing fence posts and bushes or simply inhal-
ing the breeze. Each breath brings the dog messages
from the world around him that we aren't aware of;
and it can be frustrating sometimes. What smells so
good? What is so fascinating? If only he could tell us!

Australian Shepherds can also hear much better than
we can. Their frequency range extends higher than
ours and they can hear much fainter sounds. Another
ability that exceeds ours is the ability to determine the
origin of the sounds he hears. For example, if your
Aussie hears a sound in the grass, perhaps a mouse or
a beetle, he will stand still and very slightly turn his
head from side to side. In some way, he can use his
sense of hearing to triangulate the exact location of
that mouse or bug. Then, when he's found the right
location, he can leap and pounce, catching the prey
under his forepaws.

The Australian Shepherd's protective instincts work in
conjunction with his sensitive hearing. If your Aussie
starts barking for no apparent reason, you might want
to go see why. He has probably heard a sound that you
can't hear.

Although the Australian Shepherd uses his sense of
sight more than many other breeds (except for the
sighthounds: Afghans, Greyhounds, Borzoi, etc.) we
can still see better and longer than he can. Compared
to people, most dogs are nearsighted; in other words,
they can see well up close but lose detail farther away.
However, the Aussie's vision is very keyed to movement. As a herding dog, the Aussie needed to see the

movement of the flock of sheep or the slinking of a predator, so movement became very important.

Experts used to think that dogs saw only in black and white. Recently, however, researchers tested several dogs using a computer and found that dogs can see color—not the range that people see, but instead a limited range of colors, much like a color-blind person. Up to this point, researchers simply didn't know how to determine what the dogs were seeing. Understanding that dogs see color opens up an entirely new vista in our understanding of dogs, and research is continuing to discover exactly how well they do see.

An Intelligent Dog

The Australian Shepherd is a very intelligent dog. Some people assume that an intelligent dog will always know how to behave. More often than not, an intelligent dog will find different ways to do things, many times because he gets bored more easily. For example, if you teach the average dog to go get the morning newspaper, the dog will probably go get the paper every morning, doing the same thing day after day. The Aussie, however, will quickly get bored with that routine and will try and figure out how to add some ruffles and flourishes to the morning ritual. Perhaps he will pick up the paper by one end, or by the rubber band. Perhaps he will make three dashes around the car and then get the paper. Maybe he will play keep-away after getting the paper.

A DOG'S SENSES

Sight: With their eyes located farther apart than ours, dogs can detect movement at a greater distance than we can, but they can't see as well up close. They can also see better in less light, but can't distinguish many colors.

Sound: Dogs can hear about four times better than we can, and they can hear high-pitched sounds especially well. Their ancestors, the wolves, howled to let other wolves know where they were; our dogs do the same, but they have a wider range of vocalizations, including barks, whimpers, moans and whines.

Smell: A dog's nose is his greatest sensory organ. His sense of smell is so great he can follow a trail that's weeks old, detect odors diluted to one-millionth the concentration we'd need to notice them, even sniff out a person under water!

Taste: Dogs have fewer taste buds than we do, so they're likelier to try anything—and usually do, which is why it's especially important for their owners to monitor their food intake. Dogs are omnivores, which means they eat meat as well as vegetable matter like grasses and weeds.

Touch: Dogs are social animals and love to be petted, groomed and played with.

The Aussie will show his intelligence in other ways. Some have learned how to open cupboard doors and the refrigerator, have taught themselves to turn on the water spigot in the backyard and many other things their owners probably wished they hadn't learned! The Aussie is always thinking and, for some owners, that is frightening because you really should be smarter than your dog!

Playing Frisbee with your Aussie is a good way to enjoy your dog and make sure he is getting plenty of exercise.

Because of the Aussie's drive to work and his high intelligence, obedience training is a *necessity.* This training will help establish (and reinforce) the dog-owner relationship and will give your Aussie a challenge. Dog sports are also good challenges, especially the active sports, such as Frisbee, agility and flyball. Chapters 8 and 9 discuss training and dog sports in more detail.

AUSSIE ACTIVITY LEVEL

The Australian Shepherd is a fairly high-energy dog who requires daily exercise—daily strenuous exercise. A two or three mile walk around the neighborhood might be adequate exercise for a young puppy or an older dog, but cannot be considered exercise for a healthy adult. A good fast run, a fast session of throwing the ball or a jog alongside a bicycle is more appropriate.

As mentioned earlier, the Australian Shepherd's drive to work can turn destructive if the dog doesn't have a job to do. The same thing can happen when the dog doesn't get enough exercise. Many Aussies will pace, run the fences, bark, chew, or try to escape from the yard when they are alone, bored and have an excess of energy. However, when your Aussie gets enough exercise on a daily basis, your dog will be healthier, happier and more relaxed, and destructiveness around the house and yard will be decreased.

Hair, Hair and More Hair!

Aussies shed. There is no way around it. That lush, thick silky coat does shed. If dog hair in the house bothers you, don't get an Aussie. Australian Shepherd owners deal with the problem in different ways. Some vacuum daily, others buy carpet that matches the dog's coat, others pull up the carpet and put down tile. Living with a dog requires some compromises, and dealing with dog hair without complaining is one of them.

However, you can take measures to keep shedding under control. The worst shedding times are spring and fall, depending upon the climate, but some shedding takes place all year round. The easiest way to keep it under control is to brush the dog thoroughly every day. See Chapter 6, "Grooming Your Australian Shepherd" for more detail, but it is important to note shedding here because it affects how you live with your dog.

Training your Aussie to do challenging work is a good way to keep him in top shape physically and mentally. This one is performing in open agility.

Neat and Clean

Other than shedding, Aussies are very clean dogs. Most house-train very easily and will relieve themselves in one spot in the yard, often in a corner or up against a bush. Most will walk around a pile of feces, not wanting to even touch it. Aussies do not drool, and their personal habits are very clean. Their silky coat sheds dirt easily and even a muddy Aussie will be fairly clean after drying and a brushing.

A well-trained, well-exercised dog will be a calm, quiet household companion, happy to be close to you as you read or watch television.

MORE INFORMATION ON THE AUSTRALIAN SHEPHERD

NATIONAL BREED CLUB

Australian Shepherd Club of America
6091 East State Highway 21
Bryan, TX 77803-9652

The club can provide you with breed information, an application for membership and referral to a breed club in your area.

BOOKS

Hartnagle, Joseph. *Australian Shepherds*. TFH Publications, Neptune City, NJ: 1990.

Palika, Liz. *The Australian Shepherd: Champion of Versatility*. Howell Book House, New York: 1995.

VIDEOS

American Kennel Club, *The Australian Shepherd*.

USEFUL ORGANIZATIONS

In addition to those listed in chapter 13, the following organizations may be of interest to you and your Aussie.

Canine Eye Registration Foundation (CERF)
Veterinary Medical Data Program
South Campus Courts, Building C
Purdue University
West Lafayette, IN 47907

Friskies Canine Frisbee Disc Championships
4060 Peachtree Drive, Suite 326G
Atlanta, GA 30319

American Herding Breed Association
1548 Victoria Way
Pacifica, CA 94044

WORLD WIDE WEB

Check out the following addresses for up to the minute information on Australian Shepherds.

http://www.everett.net/users/jimmb/aussie/html

http://www.asca.org/

http://ng.netgate.net/~frankb/pasa/

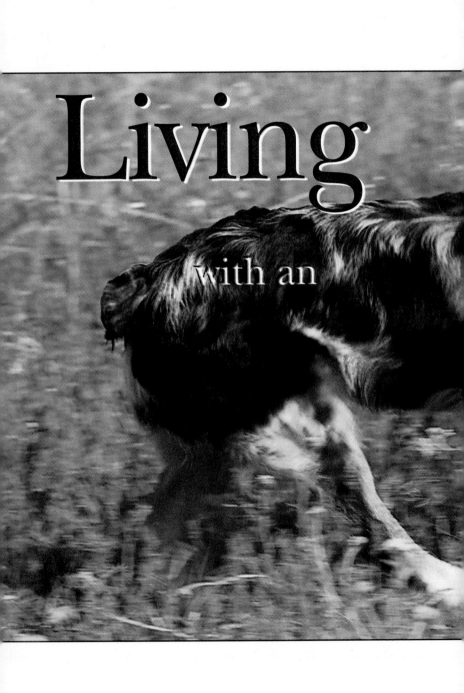

Living

with an

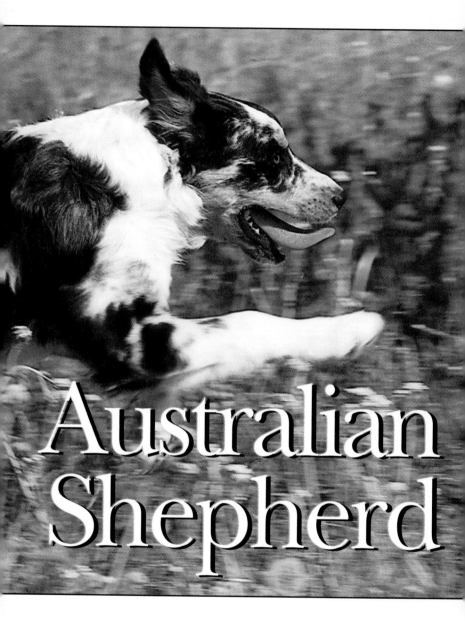

part two

Australian Shepherd

chapter 4

Bringing Your Australian Shepherd Home

First Things First

Before you bring your Australian Shepherd home, you will need some supplies; you don't want to have to make an emergency run to the store at midnight because you forgot something. Most of these are basic necessities for both the puppy and the adopted adult.

FOOD

Obviously, you will need dog food. Find out what the puppy is eating now and get some of the same food. If you wish to switch to a different brand, do so over an extended period of time so your Australian Shepherd can adjust. Rapid changes in diet can result in an upset stomach and diarrhea.

FOOD AND WATER DISHES

You will need a bowl for food and a bowl for water. The food bowl can be just about anything; some people like plastic, others like ceramic or stainless steel. Whatever you use should be large enough to hold four to six cups of food and should be easily cleaned. Some people keep the dog's water bowl outside since many Australian Shepherd puppies like to play and splash in their water. If you do keep the bowl outside, make sure it is large enough to hold 2 to 3 gallons of water and that it is unspillable. Change the water and clean the bowl daily. If yourAustralian Shepherd likes to splash in it, check it a couple times a day to make sure the dog doesn't go thirsty.

Your Aussie won't have a problem accepting leash training if you introduce her to it when she is young.

LEASH AND COLLAR

You will also need a collar and leash for your new Aussie. A buckle collar, either with a metal buckle or the plastic quick release closure, is good for both puppies and adult dogs. Adjustable collars are available that can be made larger as the puppy grows.

When you start dog training classes with your Australian Shepherd, your instructor may ask that you use a different collar. There are many different types of training collars on the market, and your instructor can give you some guidance about what might work better for you and your dog.

ID TAG

You will want an identification tag for your dog's buckle collar. This tag should include your name and both a daytime and evening telephone number. You can order this tag prior to picking up your dog so you have it ready when the dog arrives, or you can use one of the temporary tags available in many pet stores. With these tags, you write the information on a piece of paper which is then sealed inside a plastic case and attached to the dog's collar. Later, when you have your dog and have chosen a name, you can order a metal tag with your dog's name on it.

CRATE

Your new Aussie will need a kennel crate to use as a bed, a place of refuge and a place for quiet time. This crate can be the plastic kind like airlines require, or it can be a heavy metal wire cage. The style is up to you, but the crate should be large enough for an adult Australian Shepherd to stand up, turn around and lay down in comfortably.

TOYS

Puppies love toys! Have a good supply ready when you welcome your puppy to her new home.

Last, but certainly not least, you will need some toys for your Australian Shepherd. If you are going to be bringing home a new puppy, the toys should be something the puppy can chew on because very shortly she will start teething and will have a driving need to chew. Many dog owners like to offer rawhides (cured beef hide), while others like to give their dogs hard rubber toys to chew on. Again, it's your choice (and of course, your dog's). Do try to stay away from soft plastic toys, especially those with squeakers inside. Small pieces can easily be ripped off and swallowed, and could get lodged in the dog's windpipe or intestines.

If you are bringing home an older puppy or adult Aussie, offer larger rawhides or indestructible toys as Australian Shepherds have incredibly strong jaws. Ask at your local pet store what they have available.

Preparing Your Home

Prior to bringing home your Australian Shepherd, you will need to make sure your house is ready. First of all, set up the crate in your bedroom. Many people take away the nightstand next to their bed and put the crate right there. This way your dog will spend six to eight hours close to you and can smell and hear you all night long. This is a great way to bond with the dog and reassure her as she adjusts to her new home. Also, if the puppy needs to go outside during the night, you will hear her whine and cry before there is an accident.

Next, decide where your dog will spend her days. If you are home all day, this is not as big of a problem as you can supervise the puppy when she's out and about. When you can't watch the pup, you can put her in her crate. However, if you work away from home, you will need a secure place for the dog to stay while you are gone, preferably outside.

Puppies get into everything, so make sure dangerous objects are out of reach.

If you will be leaving your Australian Shepherd outside, you might want to build a secure run or exercise area. Make sure the dog won't be able to climb or dig out of it and that other dogs, coyotes or predators can't get in. Your dog will need a house and shelter from the weather and an unspillable water bowl.

PUPPYPROOFING YOUR HOME

Next, you must make sure your house, yard and garage are safe for your new Australian Shepherd. It's amazing what an inquisitive puppy or bored adult dog can get into. In the house, crawl around on your hands and knees and look at things from a dog's viewpoint. Are there dangling electrical cords that might be fun to chew on? Are books or knickknacks within reach? Are VCR tapes stored at eye level? Pick up or put away anything that looks even remotely interesting. Start teaching family members to close closet doors, pick up dirty clothes and put away shoes and slippers. With a young puppy or a new dog in the house, keeping temptation out of reach is imperative.

If your Australian Shepherd will have access to the garage, make sure all chemicals, paints and car parts are up high out of reach. Antifreeze especially is very poisonous and dogs seem to like the taste. You may even want to fence off part of the garage so there is absolutely no access to storage areas. Four by 8-foot framed wooden lattice is available at most lumber stores and makes great temporary dividers.

In the yard, look for possible escape routes—places where your dog could go under or over the fence. A pile of lumber or a rabbit hutch next to the fence could provide an easy escape route. A drainage ditch running under the fence could do the same thing. Again, try to look at your yard from the dog's point of view.

Put away garden tools, fertilizers, pesticides and pool supplies. If you have potted plants, pick them up before your Australian Shepherd turns them into play toys. Check the list of poisonous plants to make sure your landscaping and potted plants are safe just in case your dog does try to sample them. Some outside dangers include daffodils, holly, wisteria, and periwinkle. Inside the house, make sure your Aussie steers clear of amaryllis, philodendron, ivy and poinsettia.

HOUSEHOLD DANGERS

Curious puppies and inquisitive dogs get into trouble not because they are bad, but simply because they want to investigate the world around them. It's our job to protect our dogs from harmful substances, like the following:

IN THE HOUSE

cleaners, especially pine oil

perfumes, colognes, aftershaves

medications, vitamins

office and craft supplies

electric cords

chicken or turkey bones

chocolate

some house and garden plants, like ivy, oleander and poinsettia

IN THE GARAGE

antifreeze

garden supplies, like snail and slug bait, pesticides, fertilizers, mouse and rat poisons

An Australian Shepherd in the House

SETTING UP A SCHEDULE

Dogs are creatures of habit and thrive on a regular routine that doesn't vary too much from day to day. Puppies, especially, need a routine. At eight weeks of age, puppies sleep a lot. Your puppy will eat, relieve herself, play and sleep, and a couple of hours later will repeat the whole cycle. However, as she gets older, she will gradually sleep less and play more. As she learns and develops bowel and bladder control, she will go longer periods between needing to relieve herself— from every couple of hours to every three or four hours.

Puppies thrive on good care and plenty of attention and affection.

A sample schedule might look like this:

6:00am. Dad gets up and goes outside with Puppy. Praises Puppy for relieving herself, then puts Puppy back in her crate.

7:00am. Mom gets up, lets Puppy outside again and gets Junior up to get ready for school. After Junior leaves for school, Mom feeds Puppy breakfast, plays with Puppy for a few minutes and then

45

puts Puppy in her pen outside, giving Puppy a couple of chew toys. Mom leaves for work.

Noon. A neighbor comes over, lets Puppy out of the pen, plays with Puppy for a few minutes and offers Puppy lunch. After Puppy has eaten and relieved herself, the neighbor sits down and cuddles Puppy for a few minutes, plays some more and then puts Puppy back in the pen.

3:00pm. Junior comes home from school and lets Puppy out of the pen. Junior lets Puppy relieve herself, then brings Puppy inside with him. They play, cuddle and, while Junior works on his homework, Puppy chews on a toy.

5:00pm. After finishing his homework, Junior takes Puppy for a walk.

6:00pm. Mom and Dad come home from work and both greet Puppy. Junior takes Puppy outside to relieve herself.

7:00pm. After Puppy has eaten dinner and relieved herself, Dad gets down on the living room floor with Puppy and grooms her, teaching the puppy to accept brushing, combing and nail trimming and at the same time, checking her ears and so on. After grooming her, Dad plays ball with the pup.

10:00pm. Dad takes Puppy outside to relieve herself and then crates the puppy for the night.

This is, of course, a sample schedule. Your household routine will dictate what timetable you will set up.

THINKING AHEAD

Many of the commonly seen problems with dogs can be avoided through simple prevention. Puppyproofing your house is one means of prevention; make sure plants and cords are up out of the way and closet doors are closed.

Supervising the dog is another means of prevention. Your Australian Shepherd can't chew up your sofa if you supervise her while she's in the house with you and if you put her in her crate or outside in her pen when you can't watch her. By supervising the dog, you can teach her what is allowed and what is not. If your Australian Shepherd puppy decides to take a nibble out of the sofa cushion and you are paying attention, you can tell the puppy, "Acck! No!" as she grabs the cushion. Then, follow through by handing your puppy one of her chew toys: "Here, chew on this instead." You have prevented potential damage and at the same time, taught your dog what she should chew.

QUALITY TIME IS A MUST

Australian Shepherds are very people-oriented dogs and must spend time with their owners. Your dog should be inside with you when you are home and should be next to your bed at night. In addition, you will need to make time to play with your dog, train her and make sure that she gets enough exercise.

With a little thought, it's amazing how creative people can be with their

Quality time with the people they love is a must for puppies.

schedules. To spend time with your dog in the morning, getting up thirty minutes earlier will give you time for a fifteen- to twenty-minute walk before taking your shower. If you work close to home, your lunch hour might be just enough time to get home and eat your lunch as you throw the Frisbee for your dog. In the evening, take the children with you as you walk the dog; you can find out what's going on with the kids as you exercise and train your dog.

47

Crate Training

Adding a puppy to your household can be a wonderful experience, but it can sour quickly if the puppy is ruining your carpets and chewing up your shoes. There is a training tool that can help—a crate. Two types of crates are commonly used. The first is a heavy plastic molded carrier much like those the airlines require. The second is made of heavy metal wire bars. The choice of which to use is strictly personal preference, but whatever you choose should be large enough for an adult Australian Shepherd to stand up, turn around and lay down in.

A crate allows you to use the dog's natural denning instincts; the instinct that makes dogs curl up behind the chair or under a table when they nap. Puppies also have a natural instinct not to soil (relieve themselves in) the place where they sleep. A crate helps housetrain a puppy by using that instinct.

Introduce the crate by opening the door and tossing a treat or toy inside. Allow the puppy to come and go as she pleases, and to investigate the crate. When she is going in after the treat or toy, give her a treat and close the door. Leave the door closed for a few minutes and then let the puppy out if, and only if, the puppy is being quiet. If the puppy is throwing a temper tantrum, don't let her out. If you do, you will have taught your puppy that a temper tantrum works.

Put the puppy in her crate when you are home and can't supervise her or when you are busy, such as eating a meal. Put the puppy in the crate when she is over-stimulated—time outs are good for puppies, too. And of course, put the puppy in her crate for the night.

Never leave the puppy in the crate longer than four hours except at night when the crate is next to your bed. It takes a while for the puppy to develop good bowel and bladder control and you need to be able to let the puppy out when it is time.

chapter 5

Feeding
Your
Australian
Shepherd

The Importance of Good Nutrition

A healthy Australian Shepherd has bright alert eyes and a shiny coat and gives the impression of restrained power and energy. Although good health comes from many things, including the dog's genetic heritage, overall care and environment, good nutrition is vitally important to good health.

Many dogs can carry on for a long time on a substandard diet; in fact, it's amazing how well some dogs do live on scraps, garbage and whatever is tossed their way. But as with all dogs, the Australian Shepherd's body requires certain substances which he cannot manufacture himself; he must get these from the food he eats. Eventually, poor nutrition shows up as skin problems, a dull, dry coat, poor stools, behavior problems, immune system deficiencies, susceptibility to disease and eventually, a much shorter life span.

Good nutrition is important from day one.

What is Nutrition?

Nutrition is a constant process that starts at conception and ends only at death. In the *Basic Guide to Canine Nutrition,* published by Gaines Professional Services, nutrition is defined as "the process of assimilating food for the biochemical process of living." In other words, anything the dog ingests and digests gives him some kind of nutrition which his body then uses to carry out necessary biological processes. However, a food's digestibility and how the dog's body uses that food determine the amount of nutrition gained, and that can vary greatly from food to food.

NUTRITIONAL BUILDING BLOCKS

Proteins

Proteins are a varied group of biological compounds and affect many different functions in your Aussie's body, including the immune system, cell structure and growth. As true omnivores, dogs can digest protein from many different sources. The most common are meats, cooked grains, dairy products and legumes.

Dr. Ben Sheffy, Professor of Nutrition at Cornell University, suggests that puppies should eat a diet consisting of twenty-four percent digestible protein. Pregnant bitches, working adult dogs or active young adults should eat twenty percent protein; nonworking adults should eat sixteen percent protein.

Carbohydrates

Carbohydrates, like proteins, have many functions in the dog's body, including serving as structural components of cells. However, the most important function is serving as an energy source. Carbohydrates can be found in grains and other plants. The most common sources of carbohydrates include potatoes, rice, noodles and other pastas and cereal products. Dr Sheffy recommends a forty-four percent carbohydrate diet for nonworking adult dogs, a thirty-eight percent diet for working adults, pregnant bitches and young adults, and thirty-two percent for puppies.

Fats

Fats have many uses in the body. They are the most important form of energy storage, contribute to cell structure and are vital to the absorption of several different vitamins. Certain fats are also beneficial to keeping the skin and coat healthy. Fats in dog foods are found primarily in meat and dairy products. Recommended levels are ten percent for nonworking adult dogs, twelve percent for working dogs, young adults and pregnant bitches and fourteen percent for puppies.

Vitamins

Contrary to popular belief, vitamins do not supply energy but rather are vital elements necessary for growth and the maintenance of life. There are two classes of vitamins: water soluble and fat soluble. Water soluble vitamins include the B and B complex vitamins, C, thiamin, riboflavin, biotin and folic acid. Fat soluble vitamins include A, D, E and K. Vitamins A, E and B are all important to fighting disease and maintaining a strong immune system.

The B vitamins serve a number of different functions, including the metabolism of carbohydrates and amino acids. The B vitamins are integral to many biochemical functions, and deficiencies can show up as weight loss, slow growth, dry, flaky skin or even anemia, depending upon the specific deficiency. The B vitamins can be obtained from meat and dairy products.

Vitamin C is a controversial vitamin. Some respected sources state that C is not a required dietary vitamin for dogs, yet others regard C as a miracle vitamin for dogs much as it has been for people. Some feel it can help prevent hip dysplasia and other potential problems but these claims have not been proven. If you decide to give your dog vitamin C, it is water soluble and if your dog's body does not metabolize it, it will be discarded in the urine and therefore, will not hurt the dog. However, check with your vet first before considering any course of supplementation.

Vitamin A deficiencies show up as slow or retarded growth and reproductive failure, as well as skin and vision problems. The green and yellow vegetables are the best sources of vitamin A, as are carrots, fish oils and animal livers.

Minerals

Minerals, like vitamins, are necessary for life and physical well-being. Minerals can affect the body in many ways. A deficiency of calcium can lead to rickets; a deficiency of manganese can cause reproductive failure and a zinc deficiency can lead to growth retardation and skin problems.

Many minerals are tied in with vitamins; in other words, a vitamin deficiency will also result in a mineral deficiency. For example, an adequate amount of vitamin B_{12} insures there is also an adequate amount of cobalt because cobalt, a mineral, is a constituent of B_{12}.

Water

It may seem like common sense to say that your Australian Shepherd needs water, but the importance of water cannot be emphasized enough. Water makes up about seventy percent of a dog's weight. Water facilitates the generation of energy, the transportation of nutrients and the disposal of wastes. Water is in the blood stream, in the eyes, in the cerebrospinal fluid and in the gastrointestinal tract. Directly or indirectly, water is vital to all of the body's functions.

Commercial Dog Foods

Dog food in the United States is a huge business with tremendous competition among manufacturers. This is wonderful for dog owners, as the competition has created a number of feeding alternatives.

The major dog food companies have research departments that are constantly searching for ways to satisfy the dog owner and the dog. Most dog owners look at the ingredients of the dog food first. Next is the list of protein, carbohydrate and fat percentages. By offering a number of different foods, manufacturers hope to have a food to fit every owner's requirements.

Research is also continuing to determine the needs of dogs at different times of their lives. What do puppies need for good growth and development? What do more sedentary senior dogs need? What about pregnant or lactating bitches? What do dogs with allergies or illnesses require? There are foods for every stage of the dog's life, from puppy through senior citizen, including foods for allergic or ill dogs. All of this expensive research is aimed at providing better nutrition for dogs throughout their lives.

LOOK FOR GOOD QUALITY

A good quality food is necessary for your Australian Shepherd's health. Dog foods on the market today vary in quality from the very good to the terrible. To make sure you are

---

HOW TO READ THE DOG FOOD LABEL

With so many choices on the market, how can you be sure you are feeding the right food to your dog? The information is all there on the label—if you know what you're looking for.

Look for the nutritional claim right up top. Is the food "100% nutritionally complete"? If so, it's for nearly all life stages; "growth and maintenance," on the other hand, is for early development; puppy foods are marked as such, as are foods for senior dogs.

Ingredients are listed in descending order by weight. The first three or four ingredients will tell you the bulk of what the food contains. Look for the highest-quality ingredients, like meats and grains, to be among them.

The Guaranteed Analysis tells you what levels of protein, fat, fiber and moisture are in the food, in that order. While these numbers are meaningful, they won't tell you much about the quality of the food. Nutritional value is in the dry matter, not the moisture content.

In many ways, seeing is believing. If your dog has bright eyes, a shiny coat, a good appetite and a good energy level, chances are his diet's fine. Your dog's breeder and your veterinarian are good sources of advice if you're still confused.

feeding your dog a good quality food, read the labels on the dog food packages. Make sure the food offers the levels of protein, carbohydrates and fats recommended earlier in this chapter. Dog foods are a perfect example of the adage "You get what you pay for."

The end result of a diet of poor dog food is an unhealthy dog with large, foul-smelling stools and higher veterinary bills. It is much better for you and your dog to feed your dog a higher quality food all the time.

READ THE INGREDIENTS

Read the list of ingredients. If one of the first ingredients listed is "byproducts," be leery of the food. Dog food manufacturers can meet protein requirements for food by including byproducts such as hair, feathers, hooves, feet, beaks, diseased tissues and other inferior forms of protein. Australian Shepherds do well on a dog food that uses meat and bone meal as the first two or three ingredients. Steer away from foods with a lot of soy or soy products as these are thought to contribute to stomach gas which can lead to bloat. (See Chapter 7, "Keeping Your Australian Shepherd Healthy.") Some Aussies also have allergies to wheat, so you may wish to avoid wheat based dry foods.

DRY OR CANNED?

Dog foods traditionally come in two different forms: dry or canned. The raw materials for dry foods are mixed together, forced through an extruder (which gives them their shape) then baked or dried. Canned foods are cooked at a high temperature and then sealed in cans.

The water or moisture content of canned food is much higher, as is the meat content. For that reason, most dogs, when given a choice, prefer canned food over dry. Although ounce for ounce the costs may be comparable, the cost of canned food is much higher than that of dry food when you compare the nutrition value of the food. A great deal of canned food is water, which makes no nutritional contribution.

Dry food is preferred by many dog owners because it has a longer shelf life, is more easily stored, costs less and provides their dogs with tooth and gum exercise. As an added attraction, one Australian Shepherd owner said, "Dry food also smells better to me. I know my dog loves the smell of canned food but I don't!" In addition, feeding a diet of dry food dramatically increases your dog's dental health. The rough food scrapes along the teeth and gums, removing tartar and stimulating gums. The *Journal of the American Veterinary Medical Association* published an article stating that dogs fed a diet of canned food developed gum disease much earlier in life than did dogs fed a hard kibble diet. The dry food did not eliminate the need for regular dental care, but it helped prevent gum problems.

> ## HOW MANY MEALS A DAY?
>
> Individual dogs vary in how much they should eat to maintain a desired body weight—not too fat, but not too thin. Puppies need several meals a day, while older dogs may need only one. Determine how much food keeps your adult dog looking and feeling her best. Then decide how many meals you want to feed with that amount. Like us, most dogs love to eat, and offering two meals a day is more enjoyable for them. If you're worried about overfeeding, make sure you measure correctly and abstain from adding tidbits to the meals.
>
> Whether you feed one or two meals, only leave your dog's food out for the amount of time it takes her to eat it—10 minutes, for example. Freefeeding (when food is available any time) and leisurely meals encourage picky eating. Don't worry if your dog doesn't finish all her dinner in the allotted time. She'll learn she should.

Very young puppies and older senior dogs may benefit from softer food, perhaps a little kibble softened in water or meat juice to make it more palatable and easier to chew. Otherwise, Australian Shepherds will thrive on a high quality dry dog food.

Homemade Diets

Dog owners who feed homemade diets usually do so because they are concerned about the quality of commercially available foods. Some owners do not want their dogs eating the additives or preservatives that are in many commercial dog foods. Others cook their dogs' food so they can control exactly what their dogs eat.

Breeder Amy Caan has ten Australian Shepherds and cooks her own dog food. "My first Aussie had a lot of skin problems and when we had him tested, we found that he was allergic to wheat, beef, lamb and soy as well as a number of other things. It's very hard to find a good quality dog food that doesn't have some or all of these ingredients so I consulted with a couple of different allergists, dietitians and doctors and made up my own diet." Her allergic dog is now twelve years old and in good health and her other Australian Shepherds are on the same diet.

One of the biggest problems with a homemade diet is ensuring that it is a balanced diet. Years of research have gone into most commercial diets, and there is no way we can duplicate that work. If you decide you want to cook for your Australian Shepherd, talk to your veterinarian first, he or she might want to refer you to a nutritional specialist.

Feeding Your Australian Shepherd

FREEFEED OR SET TIMES?

Many dog owners like to fill a bowl of dog food and leave it out all day, letting the dog munch at will. Although it may be convenient, it is not a good idea for several reasons. First of all, the bowl of food attracts birds, squirrels and ants. When you are housetraining your puppy, freefeeding makes it difficult to set up a routine. Your puppy will need to relieve himself after eating and if he munches all day long, you won't be able to tell when he should go outside.

TYPES OF FOODS/TREATS

There are three types of commercially available dog food—dry, canned and semimoist—and a huge assortment of treats (lucky dogs!) to feed your dog. Which should you choose?

Dry and canned foods contain similar ingredients. The primary difference between them is their moisture content. The moisture is not just water. It's blood and broth, too, the very things that dogs adore. So while canned food is more palatable, dry food is more economical, convenient and effective in controlling tartar buildup. Most owners feed a 25% canned/75% dry diet to give their dogs the benefit of both. Just be sure your dog is getting the nutrition he needs (you and your veterinarian can determine this).

Semimoist foods have the flavor dogs love and the convenience owners want. However, they tend to contain excessive amounts of artificial colors and preservatives.

Dog treats come in every size, shape and flavor imaginable, from organic cookies shaped like postmen to beefy chew sticks. Dogs seem to love them all, so enjoy the variety. Just be sure not to overindulge your dog. Factor treats into her regular meal sizes.

Last, but certainly not least, your dog needs to know that you are the giver of the food and how better for him to learn it than for you to hand him a bowl twice a day? If the food is always available, your puppy won't realize it's coming from you.

How Much?

Each and every Australian Shepherd needs a different amount of food. The dog's individual body metabolism, activity rate and lifestyle all affect his nutrition needs.

Make sure there is always plenty of fresh, clean water available for your Australian Shepherd.

Most dog food manufacturers have on the dog food bag a chart showing how much to feed your dog. It's important to note that these are *suggested* guidelines. If your puppy or dog is soft, round and fat, cut back on the food. If your dog is thin and is always hungry, increase the portion size.

Mealtimes

Feed your Australian Shepherd after you have eaten. Again, this may not seem important to you, but in a dog's world, the most dominant dog would eat first. Since your Aussie must see you as the boss, the equivalent of the dominant dog, you need to eat first.

Most experts recommend that puppies eat two to three times a day and adult dogs eat once or twice a day. Most

57

dogs do very well with two meals, ten to twelve hours apart. Feed your dog after you eat breakfast and then again after you have dinner.

While you are eating, don't feed your Australian Shepherd from the table or toss him scraps. Not only will this weaken your position as the dominant family member, but it will cause him to beg from anyone at the table; a very bad habit.

SNACKS AND TREATS

An occasional dog biscuit or training treat will not spoil your Australian Shepherd's appetite, but don't get in the habit of offering too many treats. Many American dogs are overweight and obesity is a leading killer of dogs. When you do offer treats, offer either tidbits made specifically for dogs or something low-calorie and nutritious, like a carrot. Don't offer candy, cookies, left-over tacos or anything like that. Your Australian Shepherd doesn't need sugar, chocolate is deadly for dogs and spicy foods will cause diarrhea and an upset stomach. Play it safe and give your Australian Shepherd good quality, nutritious snacks sparingly.

Grooming
Your
Australian
Shepherd

Good grooming is necessary not only to keep your dog looking her best, but also for good health. A regular grooming routine will keep you in touch with your dog and enable you to detect anything out of the ordinary, including parasites, foreign objects stuck in the coat and skin conditions.

Coat Care

The Australian Shepherd's wonderful coat helps make her a versatile working dog, able to function in just about any climate. This double coat, with silky outer guard hair and a thick, softer undercoat, is also easy to keep up. It does not matte (tangle into knots), nor does it need to be trimmed.

This coat does have a drawback, though. It sheds! Australian Shepherds shed heavily twice a year; normally in the spring and fall, although the exact time depends upon your climate and the dog's living conditions. However, the coat sheds a little all the time, all year round. Regular coat care will help to reduce shedding on furniture and carpet.

BRUSHING

If you brush your Australian Shepherd thoroughly two to three times a week, you can keep the hair on the floor and carpet to a minimum. There are three grooming tools that you should use when brushing your Australian Shepherd.

A **pin brush** looks like a woman's hair brush. It usually has an oval head with numerous metal bristles. This brush will go through the coat down to the skin and will loosen clumps of coat, dirt, grass seeds, burrs or other debris. Use this brush first.

A well groomed Aussie is a pleasure to look at.

To brush your dog, lay her on her side and sit or kneel next to her so that you can both relax. Then, starting at the head, brush the direction that the coat grows. Brush with the coat, from the head down to the nub of the tail. Then roll your dog over and do the same thing on the other side.

The next tool you will use is a **shedding blade.** This looks like a flexible saw blade bent into a U-shape with a handle holding both blades together. This does not go through the coat but instead will pull out the dead coat. With your dog still laying on her side, repeat your previous pattern, going over the dog from head to tail on each side.

You will finish by going over the dog completely with a **slicker brush.** This will gather all the loose coat the other brushes left behind. Follow the same pattern. You may wish to introduce your dog to the canister vacuum. If she will tolerate it, this is of tremendous help getting the last shedding coat off the dog.

When you're done brushing your Australian Shepherd, you should have a dog with a clean shiny coat and a garbage bag (or vacuum bag) full of loose hair.

BATHING

Depending on your Australian Shepherd's living environment, you may wish to bathe her once a week or once a month. If your dog is a working therapy dog, visiting nursing homes and hospitals, she will need to be bathed prior to each visit. If your dog helps herd sheep and then stays inside at night, she'll need to be bathed often. On the other hand, if your dog lives in the house with you and rarely plays in messy outside environments, she may stay clean and odor-free for weeks at a time. It doesn't matter how often you bathe your dog—even weekly won't hurt her—as long as you use a shampoo formulated for dogs that is gentle and conditioning.

Grooming is an opportunity to give your dog a relaxing massage.

When choosing a shampoo, ask your veterinarian or a dog groomer for his or her recommendations; there are so many shampoos on the market. When you buy the shampoo, read the instructions carefully. Some shampoos are to be diluted in water, a capful or half a cup to a gallon of water. Other shampoos, especially those formulated to kill fleas or ticks, must remain on the dog for two to five minutes before being rinsed off. To make sure you use the shampoo correctly, read the entire label.

You can bathe your dog outside if the weather is warm and the water from your hose isn't too cold, or

you can bathe her in the bathtub. Either way, change into old clothes (you will get wet!) and leash your dog. Put a cotton ball in each of your dog's ears to keep water out. Make sure she is thoroughly brushed first and then use the hose or shower to get her entirely wet. It can be hard sometimes to wet the dog clear to the skin; that wonderful double coat repels water well.

Once your Australian Shepherd is wet, put some shampoo on your hands and start working into the coat, starting at the head and ears and

Use a shedding blade to remove dead hair.

working down the neck. Be careful not to get soap in her eyes. Continue until the dog is covered with shampoo; don't forget her legs, tummy, groin and tail. Rinse in the same manner, starting at her head and working down the body. Rinse thoroughly; any soap left on her body could make her itch and even cause a rash.

If you live in an area where fleas and ticks are prevalent and you need to dip your dog, make sure you read and follow the directions carefully. Dips are insecticides and, as such, are poisonous. Used improperly, they can cause you or your dog great harm, so be careful. (If you need some help or are worried about using insecticides properly, call a local dog groomer and have him or her dip your dog.)

Once your Australian Shepherd is thoroughly rinsed, let her shake off the excess water; then, before you towel her off, go get your canister vacuum. Put the hose on the air exit port so the vacuum is blowing air instead of sucking air, and use that air stream to blow the excess water off your dog. Now towel dry her and if you wish, use your blow dryer to finish the job. Just be careful not to burn her with it.

Other Grooming Procedures

EAR CLEANING

Each time you brush your Australian Shepherd, you should check her ears for dirt, wax buildup and foreign objects, like foxtails, burrs or other grass seeds. Obviously, any foreign objects should be removed and if you see something you can't get to, call your veterinarian immediately. If the dog's ears have

Check your Aussie's ears as part of your usual grooming routine, and clean them when necessary.

a sour smell or seem to be extremely dirty, or if the dog is pawing at his ears or shaking his head, call your veterinarian immediately.

If the dog's ears are dirty or waxy, wet a cotton ball slightly with witch hazel and, using your finger, gently swab out the ear, getting the cotton ball into all the cracks and crevasses of the ear. You may want to use two or three cotton balls per ear.

EYE CARE

If your Australian Shepherd has some matter in the corners of his eyes, just use a damp paper towel to pick up the matter. It's just like the sleep matter you sometimes have when you wake up. However, if your dog has a different type of discharge, or his eyes are red and irritated, call your veterinarian.

DENTAL HYGIENE

If you start when your Australian Shepherd is a puppy, keeping your dog's teeth clean can be easy. Take some gauze from your first aid kit and wrap it around your index finger. Dampen it and dip it in baking soda. Take that baking soda and rub it over your dog's teeth, working gently over each tooth, the inside and the outside, and into the gum line, taking care not to hurt the dog.

The rubbing action of the rough gauze and the chemical characteristics of the baking soda will help prevent plaque formation and will get rid of the bacteria that forms on the teeth and gums. Do two or three teeth and let your dog have a drink. Then work on a couple more. You may even want to break it into several sessions, doing half or a quarter of the dog's mouth at each session.

Dr. Paul Richieri, a veterinarian from Oceanside, California, recommends daily teeth cleaning. However, if daily cleaning is not possible he recommends a thorough cleaning at least three times a week.

Good grooming contributes to winning style, in or out of the showring.

NAIL TRIMMING

Your dog's toenails need to be trimmed regularly, preferably once a week. If the nails get too long, they can actually deform the foot by applying pressure against the ground, causing the toes to be in an unnatural position. Long nails are more prone to breaking and tearing, too, and that can be as painful to the dog as it is when we tear a long fingernail.

There are two basic types of toenail clippers. One is shaped much like a pair of scissors and the other has a guillotine-type blade. The type you choose is up to you; both work well, it's simply a matter of what is comfortable for you.

With your clippers in hand, have your dog lay down on the floor in front of you. Take one foot and pull the hair back from the nail so you can see the entire nail. If your dog's nails are black, you won't be able to see the quick but if your Australian Shepherd has one or two white nails, you will be able to see the pink quick inside. If you cut into the quick when you are trimming the nails, the nail will bleed and your dog will cry. The quick is just like your nailbed and hurts just as much.

If your dog has a white nail, you can use that nail as a guide for how much to trim. However, if your dog's nails are all black, you will have to take it a little slower. Look at the nail's shape. It is arched and at the end, if the nails are long, there is a slight hook. You can safely trim that hook without hitting the quick. Then, very carefully, take just a little more.

Obviously, you will know when you hit the quick; you'll feel guilty because your dog will be crying and bleeding. Don't panic. Take a bar of soap from the bathroom and rub the nail along the soap. The soap will clog the nail for a few minutes until the blood can clot. Now, while the soap is in the nail, hold that paw and look at the nail you cut. How far did you go? Trim the other nails, using that one as a guide but taking less off of the other nails.

Many dogs dislike having their nails trimmed. Some will whine or cry so much you may even think you have cut into the quick. Other dogs will try to escape from you, fighting and wiggling. If your Australian Shepherd dislikes nail trimming, try to make it as pleasant as possible. Have the nail clippers at hand but hidden;

GROOMING TOOLS

pin brush

slicker brush

flea comb

towel

mat rake

grooming glove

scissors

nail clippers

teeth-cleaning equipment

shampoo

conditioner

clippers

perhaps in your pocket. Have your dog lay down in front of you and then give him a massage, slowly and gently. When the dog is relaxed, touch one of his feet, again, slowly and gently. Then go back to massaging. Then touch his feet again. By doing this, you are showing him that touching his feet is painless and is followed by more massaging.

When the dog will let you touch his paws without reacting, have the nail clippers in hand as you massage and then trim one nail. Just one and go back to massaging. When the dog is relaxed again, trim one more. And so on. If your dog is very frightened of nail trimming, you may want to break this down even further, doing one paw per massage session.

COMMON SENSE

A healthy Australian Shepherd should have a shiny coat, clean ears and short nails. The dog shouldn't smell or be offensive in any way. Use common sense when grooming your dog. If you are unfamiliar with a shampoo or dip, read the label. If you feel a product might be too harsh or might be dangerous, don't use it and call your veterinarian or groomer.

chapter 7

Keeping Your
Australian
Shepherd
Healthy

Your Australian Shepherd cannot take care of himself. When you took this dog home, you assumed the responsibility of caring for him. This means not just making sure he is fed and brushed, but also checking his nails, making sure vaccinations are up to date and getting him to the veterinarian when necessary. The easiest way to make sure your

dog is well cared for is to set up a routine and follow it each and every day without fail.

Preventive Health Care

Once a day, you need to run your hands over your Australian Shepherd, not just over the coat as you do when you pet your dog, but instead, run your fingers through and under the coat so you can feel the dog's skin. As you do this you will get to know the feel of your dog. Should a tick latch on and bury its head in your dog's skin, you will feel it with your fingers. If your dog cuts himself or has a lump, swelling or a skin rash, you will feel it. By checking the dog this way every day, you will find these things before they turn into bigger problems.

The best time for this exam is after you have brushed your Australian Shepherd when you and the dog will both be relaxed. Put the brushes down and, starting at the dog's head as you do with brushing, run your hands over his head, around the muzzle, over the skull, feeling around the base of the ears, through the thick neck hair, making sure you touch every square inch of skin. Take your time as you do this. Think of it as giving your dog a gentle massage. Your dog may go to sleep as you massage but make sure you don't. Stay alert and look for potential problems.

As you go over your dog, check each paw thoroughly for burrs, foxtails, thorns and cuts.

As you examine your Australian Shepherd, become familiar with every part of his body. Let your hands and fingers learn what your dog feels like. Run your hands over the shoulders, down the front legs, over the rib cage and down the back to the hips. Run your hands down each leg, handling each toe on each paw, checking for burrs and foxtails, cuts and scratches. Don't forget to run your hands down the tail, too, checking for lumps, bumps and burrs.

In chapter 6, we discussed how to clean your Australian Shepherd's teeth during regular grooming sessions. It is also important to check the teeth on a regular basis, looking for inflamed gums, foreign objects or possible cracked or broken teeth. As you massage your dog's head, open the mouth and take a look. Look at the inside and the outside of the teeth. Become familiar with what the teeth look like so you will be able to spot a problem should your dog have one in the future.

In chapter 6, we also discussed how to clean the inside of the ears, gently wiping them with cotton balls moistened with witch hazel or a commercial product made especially for cleaning the ears. You can do this after brushing your dog, before you do the massage. As you wipe out the ear, check for scratches or foreign objects and give the ear a sniff. If there is quite a bit of discharge and the ear has a sour smell, call your veterinarian as your dog may have an ear infection.

Some Australian Shepherds have skin allergies. The culprit may be a certain ingredient in the shampoo you are using, pollen from the nearby field or even an ingredient in the dog's food. Skin allergies can show up as red skin, a rash, hives or a weeping, oozing sore. If, during your daily exam, you see a skin problem starting, get your Australian Shepherd in to your veterinarian right away. It's much easier to treat a skin problem when it's first starting than it is later, when the problem has spread and the dog is tormented by the itching. Your veterinarian might also be able to help you identify the cause of the reaction.

During your daily exam, check also for cuts, scrapes, bruises and sores. If you find any minor cuts and scrapes, you can wash them off with soap and water and apply a mild antibiotic ointment. However, if a cut is gaping or looks red and inflamed, call your veterinarian.

Another benefit of this daily exam will show up when you need to take your Australian Shepherd to the veterinarian; your dog will be used to intimate handling and will not be as stressed by it as a dog that is not handled in this manner.

Infectious Diseases

The diseases listed below can all be prevented by vaccinating your Australian Shepherd, starting when he is a puppy. However, there are many factors that govern how well a dog reacts to a vaccination, including the antibodies the dog got from his mother, how the dog's own immune system reacts to the vaccine and his general state of health. In rare cases, the vaccinations may not be effective. Talk to your veterinarian about a vaccination schedule for your dog.

Distemper   Distemper is a very contagious viral disease that used to kill thousands of dogs. With the effective vaccines available today, it should not kill any dogs but unfortunately, because of carelessness or oversight, it still does occasionally.

Dogs with distemper are weak and depressed, and have a fever and a discharge from the eyes and nose. They cough, vomit and have diarrhea. Intravenous fluids and antibiotics may help support an infected dog but unfortunately, most die.

A distemper vaccination can normally prevent distemper. However, vaccinations work by stimulating the immune system. If there is a problem with the immune system or if your Australian Shepherd has not received a complete series of vaccinations, he may not be adequately protected.

Vaccinations will go a long way toward keeping your puppy healthy and disease free.

Hepatitis   Infectious canine hepatitis is a highly contagious virus that primarily attacks the liver but can also cause severe kidney damage. It is not related to the form of hepatitis that affects people. The virus is spread through contaminated saliva, mucus, urine or feces. Initial symptoms include depression, vomiting, abdominal pain, high fever and jaundice. Mild cases may be treated with intravenous fluids, antibiotics and even blood transfusions. However, the mortality rate is very high. Vaccinations, usually given in conjunction with the distemper vaccine, can prevent hepatitis.

Coronavirus Coronavirus is rarely fatal to adult dogs, although it is frequently fatal to puppies. The symptoms include vomiting, loss of appetite and a yellowish, watery stool that might contain mucus or blood. The stools carry the shed virus, which is highly contagious.

Fluid or electrolyte therapy can alleviate the dehydration associated with diarrhea, but there is no treatment for the virus itself. There is a vaccine available, which is usually given in combination with the distemper, hepatitis, leptospirosis and parvo vaccinations.

> **YOUR PUPPY'S VACCINES**
>
> Vaccines are given to prevent your dog from getting an infectious disease like canine distemper or rabies. Vaccines are the ultimate preventive medicine: they're given before your dog ever gets the disease so as to protect him from the disease. That's why it is necessary for your dog to be vaccinated routinely. Puppy vaccines start at eight weeks of age for the five-in-one DHLPP vaccine and are given every three to four weeks until the puppy is sixteen months old. Your veterinarian will put your puppy on a proper schedule and will remind you when to bring in your dog for shots.

Parvovirus Parvovirus, or parvo as it is commonly known, is a terrible killer of puppies. It is a severe gastrointestinal virus that attacks the inner lining of the intestines, causing bloody diarrhea with a distinct odor. In puppies under ten weeks of age, the virus also attacks the heart and can cause death, often with no other symptoms. Parvo is so extremely contagious that is has swept through kennels and humane societies, causing multiple deaths in as little as forty-eight hours.

The gastroenteritis (inflamation of the stomach) can be treated with fluid therapy and antibiotics. However, the virus moves rapidly and dehydration can lead to shock and death in a matter of hours. There is now a vaccination for parvo which is often given combined with the distemper, hepatitis, leptospirosis and corona vaccines.

Leptospirosis Leptospirosis is a bacterial disease spread by infected wildlife. The infectious bacteria is

Living with
an Australian
Shepherd

shed in the urine. When your Australian Shepherd sniffs at a bush that has been marked with contaminated urine, or drinks from a contaminated stream, he may pick up the bacteria. The bacteria then attacks the kidneys, causing kidney failure. Unfortunately, people can also pick up lepto.

Symptoms of lepto include fever, loss of appetite, possible diarrhea and jaundice. Antibiotics can be used to treat the disease, but the outcome is usually not good due to the serious kidney and liver damage caused by the bacteria. Consideration must also be taken of the highly contagious nature of the disease to other dogs, animals and people. Dogs can receive a vaccination for lepto which is combined with the distemper, hepatitis, parvo and corona vaccinations.

Tracheobronchitis Commonly called canine cough or kennel cough, this respiratory infection can be caused by any number of different viral or bacterial agents. These highly contagious, airborne agents can cause a variety of symptoms, including inflammation of the trachea, bronchi and lungs as well as mild to severe coughing. Antibiotics may be prescribed to combat or prevent pneumonia, which may accompany the infection, and a cough suppressant may quiet the cough.

Some forms of the disease may be prevented by vaccination but there are so many strains of the disease that vaccinations alone cannot prevent tracheobronchitis. Luckily, the disease is usually mild and many dogs recover quickly without any treatment at all.

ADVANTAGES OF SPAY/NEUTER

The greatest advantage of spaying (for females) or neutering (for males) your dog is that you are guaranteed your dog will not produce puppies. There are too many puppies already available for too few homes. There are other advantages as well.

ADVANTAGES OF SPAYING

No messy heats.

No "suitors" howling at your windows or waiting in your yard.

Decreased incidences of pyometra (disease of the uterus) and breast cancer.

ADVANTAGES OF NEUTERING

Lessens male aggressive and territorial behaviors, but doesn't affect the dog's personality. Behaviors are often owner-induced, so neutering is not the only answer, but it is a good start.

Prevents the need to roam in search of bitches in season.

Decreased incidences of urogenital diseases.

Rabies Rabies is a highly infectious virus usually carried by wildlife, especially bats, raccoons and skunks, although any warm-blooded animal, including people, may become infected. The virus is transmitted through the saliva, usually through a bite or break in the skin. The virus then travels up to the brain and spinal cord and throughout the body.

Behavior changes are the first sign of the disease. Nocturnal animals will come out during the day, fearful or shy animals will become bold and aggressive or friendly and affectionate. As the virus spreads, the animal will have trouble swallowing and will drool or salivate excessively. Paralysis and convulsions follow. There is no treatment once the virus enters the brain; however, preventive vaccinations are very effective.

Spaying and Neutering

We have, unfortunately, a tremendous pet overpopulation problem in the United States today. Thousands upon thousands of dogs are destroyed each year in shelters all over the country. Many of these dogs are wonderful dogs who should have had the chance to live out their lives, but there are simply not enough homes available.

The problem has many causes and it's useless to lay blame now. However, we can prevent the problem from getting any worse in the future and hopefully lessen the numbers of dogs being destroyed. The answer is spaying and neutering. By preventing reproduction, fewer puppies are available for the limited number of homes available.

Spaying and neutering serves other purposes, as well. A male dog who has been neutered (castrated) is less likely to roam and be aggressive toward other dogs and will be less inclined to urinate to mark territory. A female dog in season (receptive to males) will attract hordes of male dogs that wish to mate her. A spayed female dog will, of course, not go through that heat season.

The health benefits of spaying and neutering are numerous. Researchers have found that spayed and neutered dogs have lower incidences of cancer later in life, up to ninety percent less. That alone is incredible. In addition, the lessened hormone drive in both males and females makes them much better companions.

BREEDING FOR THE WRONG REASONS

Many people breed, or want to breed, their dogs for the wrong reasons. One of the most common is that they love their pet and want to have a puppy to carry on. Unfortunately, a puppy from their treasured pet will not be the same. The genetic combination that created their pet was from their pets' ancestors. A puppy will be from their pet and from the dog they breed their pet to. The puppy will be an individual all unto itself.

If the owners of a treasured dog want a dog very much like the one they have, they need to go back to the breeder where they got their dog and get another one from the same lineage. That dog, too, will be an individual, but will be more like their treasured companion.

Another commonly used line of reasoning is that they wish their children to see the miracle of life. The reality, however, is that female dogs want privacy when they give birth, not an audience. In addition to that, or perhaps because of it, most puppies are born in the very early morning hours, so the kids probably won't see the miracle at all.

Many people feel that their dog should be allowed to reproduce because he (or she) is a purebred or because the dog has "papers." The fact that a dog is a registered purebred is no assurance of quality and with the population problem we are having, only the best dogs of every breed should reproduce.

The definition of "best" is the dog that compares most closely with the breed standard; that is healthy, sound, of good personality and temperament; that shows intelligence and trainability; and that has a strong desire to please. These qualities are best determined by people who know the breed very well, who have spent years studying, living with, and breeding Australian Shepherds. It's best to leave breeding in the hands of the experienced few. This helps to keep dogs from being born only to be put to sleep, and also helps ensure that only the best dogs of a given breed are reproducing to keep the breed healthy and strong.

External Parasites

FLEAS

A flea is a small insect, about the size of the head of a pin. It is crescent shaped, has six legs and is a tremendous jumper. Fleas live by biting the host animal and eating its blood.

You can see fleas by back brushing the coat and looking at the skin. A flea will appear as a tiny darting speck, trying to hide in the hair. Fleas best show up on the dog's belly, near the genitals. You can also tell by laying your dog on a solid colored sheet and brushing vigorously. If you

The flea is a die-hard pest.

see salt and pepper type residue falling to the sheet, your Australian Shepherd has fleas. The residue is made up of fecal matter (the "pepper") and eggs (the "salt").

A heavy infestation can actually kill a dog, especially the very young and very old. Keep in mind that each time a flea bites, it eats a drop or two of blood. Multiply that by numerous bites a day times the number of fleas and you can see how dangerous an infestation can be.

Fleas can also cause other problems. Many Australian Shepherds are allergic to the flea's saliva and scratch each bite until a sore develops. This flea allergy **dermatitis** is a serious problem in many areas of the country. Fleas can also carry diseases, including the infamous bubonic plague, and are the intermediary host for tapeworms.

To reduce the flea population, you need to treat the dog and his environment. If you simply treat the dog and do not treat the house, yard and car, your Australian Shepherd will simply become reinfected.

There are a number of products on the market, including strong chemical insecticides and natural botanical products. What you decide to use depends upon how bad your flea infestation is and your personal preferences. The stronger chemicals, such as organophosphates and carbamates, will kill the fleas, of course, but they can also kill birds and wildlife. You must read the directions and use them properly.

The natural products are not as strong and some do not kill the flea immediately, sometimes it takes a few hours. Some products use silica or diatonaceous earth to cut or erode the flea's shell so that it dehydrates. There are also commercial products that use natural oils, such as pennyroyal, eucalyptus or citrus, to repel the fleas. Use these products according to directions, as even natural products can be harmful when used incorrectly.

If you have any questions about what is safe to use on your dog, call your veterinarian or groomer. If you have questions about how to use a particular product, call the manufacturer. They will be more than willing to talk to you and explain exactly how the product should be used. Fleas are great survivors, and eggs can live in the environment for literally years, waiting for the right conditions to hatch. This is not an insect that can be ignored!

FIGHTING FLEAS

Remember, the fleas you see on your dog are only part of the problem—the smallest part! To rid your dog and home of fleas, you need to treat your dog *and* your home. Here's how:

• Identify where your pet(s) sleep. These are "hot spots."

• Clean your pets' bedding regularly by vacuuming and washing.

• Spray "hot spots" with a non-toxic, long-lasting flea larvicide.

• Treat outdoor "hot spots" with insecticide.

• Kill eggs on pets with a product containing insect growth regulators (IGRs).

• Kill fleas on pets per your veterinarian's recommendation.

TICKS

As you examine your Australian Shepherd, also check for ticks that may have lodged in the ears or in the hair at the base of the ear, the armpits or around the genitals. If you find a tick, a small insect about the size of a pencil eraser when engorged with blood, smear it thoroughly with Vaseline. As the tick suffocates in the Vaseline, it will back out and you can then grab it with tweezers and kill it. If the tick doesn't back out, grab it with tweezers and slowly pull it out, twisting very gently. Don't just grab and pull or the tick's head may separate from the body. If the head remains in the skin, an infection or abscess may result and veterinary treatment may be required.

Use tweezers to remove ticks from your dog.

A word of caution: don't use your fingers or fingernails to pull out ticks. Ticks can carry a number of diseases, including Lyme disease, Rocky Mountain spotted fever and a number of others, all of which can be very serious. A couple of weeks after removing ticks from her dogs (using her fingers), a friend of mine came down with viral encephalitis, a potentially serious disease. After quizzing her, her doctor felt she got the disease from the ticks. Luckily she is now okay, but a pair of tweezers would have saved her and her husband a lot of pain and worry, not to mention medical bills.

Three types of ticks (l-r): the wood tick, brown dog tick and deer tick.

Although some flea products are advertised as being able to kill ticks, too, the best way to make sure your Australian Shepherd is tick-free is to examine his body regularly. Make it part of your daily exam.

Internal Parasites

ROUNDWORMS

These long, white worms are commonly found internal parasites, especially in puppies (although they are occasionally found in adult dogs and people). The adult female roundworm can lay up to 200,000 eggs a day, which are passed out in the dog's feces. Roundworms can only be transmitted via the feces.

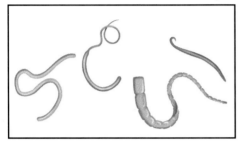

Because of this, stools should be picked up daily and your dog should be prevented from investigating other dogs' feces.

If treated early, roundworms are not serious. However, a heavy infestation can severely affect a dog's health. Puppies with roundworms will not thrive and will appear thin, with a dull coat and a pot-bellied appearance. In people, roundworms can be more serious, therefore early treatment, regular fecal checks and good sanitation are important, both for your Australian Shepherd's continued good health and yours.

Common internal parasites (l-r): roundworm, whipworm, tapeworm and hookworm.

HOOKWORMS

Hookworms live their adult lives in the small intestines of dogs. They attach to the intestinal wall and suck blood. When they detach and move to a new location, the old wound continues to bleed because of the anticoagulant the worm injects when it bites. Because of this, bloody diarrhea is usually the first sign of a problem.

Hookworm eggs are passed through the feces and are either picked up from the stools, as with roundworms, or if conditions are right, hatch in the soil and attach themselves to the feet of their new hosts, where they can burrow into the skin. After burrowing through the skin, they migrate to the intestinal tract, where the cycle starts all over again.

People can pick up hookworms by walking barefoot in infected soil. In the Sunbelt states, children often pick up hookworm eggs when playing outside in the dirt or in a sandbox. Treatment, for both dogs and people, may have to be repeated.

TAPEWORMS

Tapeworms attach to the intestinal wall to absorb nutrients. They grow by creating new segments and

usually the first sign of an infestation is the rice-like segments found in the stools or on the dog's coat near the rectum. Tapeworms are acquired when a dog chews a flea bite and swallows a flea, the intermediate host. Therefore, a good flea control program is the best way to prevent a tapeworm infestation.

WHIPWORMS

Adult whipworms live in the large intestine where they feed on blood. The eggs are passed in the stool and can live in the soil for many years. If your dog eats the fresh spring grass, or buries his bone in the yard, he can pick up eggs from the infected soil. If you garden, you can pick up eggs under your fingernails, infecting yourself if you touch your face.

Go over your dog thoroughly looking for ticks he may have picked up outside.

Heavy infestations cause diarrhea, often watery or bloody. The dog may appear thin and anemic, with poor coat. Severe bowel problems may result. Unfortunately, whipworms can be difficult to detect as the worms do not continually shed eggs. Therefore a stool sample one day may be clear while the next day may show eggs.

GIARDIA

Giardia is common in wild animals in many areas, so if you take your Aussie hiking, camping or herding, he can pick up giardia, as can you. Diarrhea is one of the first symptoms. If your dog has diarrhea and you and your dog have been out camping, make sure you tell your veterinarian where you have been.

HEARTWORMS

Adult heartworms live in the upper heart and greater pulmonary arteries where they damage the vessel walls. Poor circulation results, which in turn damages other bodily functions and eventually results in death from heart failure.

The adult worms produce thousands of tiny larvae called microfilaria. These circulate throughout the bloodstream until they are sucked up by an intermediate host, the mosquito. The microfilaria goes through the larval stages in the mosquito, then is transferred back to another dog when the mosquito bites again.

Run your hands regularly over your dog to feel for any injuries.

Dogs infected with heartworms can be treated if caught early. Unfortunately, the treatment itself can be risky and has killed some dogs. However, preventive medications are available which kill the larvae. Heartworm can be diagnosed by a blood test and a negative result is required before starting the preventive treatments.

Emergency First Aid

When you are trying to decide what is wrong with your Australian Shepherd, you will need to play detective. Your dog cannot tell you, "I have a pain right here and I feel like I'm going to throw up." You need to be observant and put the puzzle pieces together. If you call your veterinarian, he or she will also ask you some questions that you need to be able to answer.

What first caused you to think there was a problem? What was your first clue there was something wrong? Is your dog eating normally? What do his stools look like? Is he limping? When you do a hands-on exam, is the dog sore anywhere? Does he have a lump? Is anything red or swollen? Think about all of these clues and be prepared to tell your veterinarian.

Your vet will also ask you if your dog has a fever. You can take your dog's temperature using a rectal thermometer. Shake the thermometer down and then put some petroleum jelly on it. Insert the thermometer into the anus about an inch. Keep holding the thermometer, don't let go of it, and watch your clock. After three minutes, withdraw the thermometer, wipe it off and read the temperature. Normal is 101 to 102 degrees.

The veterinarian will also ask if your dog is vomiting and, if he did, what did the vomit look like? Was there anything unusual in it? Did the dog vomit up garbage? Or a plastic bag? Or grass? How often did the dog vomit? Just once or is it on-going?

Similar questions will be asked about the dog's bowel movements. Did the dog have a bowel movement? If so, did it look normal? Was there mucus or blood in the stool? Did the stool have a different or peculiar smell? Did you see any foreign objects in the stool?

A FIRST-AID KIT

Keep a canine first-aid kit on hand for general care and emergencies. Check it periodically to make sure liquids haven't spilled or dried up, and replace medications and materials after they're used. Your kit should include:

Activated charcoal tablets

Adhesive tape
(1 and 2 inches wide)

Antibacterial ointment
(for skin and eyes)

Aspirin (buffered or enteric coated, *not* Ibuprofen)

Bandages: Gauze rolls (1 and 2 inches wide) and dressing pads

Cotton balls

Diarrhea medicine

Dosing syringe

Hydrogen peroxide (3%)

Petroleum jelly

Rectal thermometer

Rubber gloves

Rubbing alcohol

Scissors

Tourniquet

Towel

Tweezers

Be prepared to answer all these questions and if you are nervous or scared, write them down.

It is often difficult for dog owners to decide when to call the veterinarian and when they can handle a problem at home. Listed below are some commonly seen problems and some basic advice about how you might handle them. However, the cost of a telephone call is small compared to your dog's life. When in doubt—call!

ANIMAL BITES

Use a scarf or old hose to make a temporary muzzle, as shown.

Muzzle your dog if he is in pain. Use a pair of panty hose or a long piece of gauze, wrap it around the dog's muzzle, crossing under the jaw, then pulling it around the dog's head, tying it in the back.

Trim the hair from around the wound and liberally pour hydrogen peroxide over it. A hand-held pressure bandage can help stop the bleeding. Stitches may be necessary if the bite is a rip or tear so call your vet; he may also recommend putting the dog on antibiotics.

If your dog has been bitten by a snake, try to get a look at the snake, making note of colors, patterns and markings so you or your vet can identify it. Keep the dog as quiet as possible to restrict the flow of venom. If the bite is on a leg, apply a tourniquet above the wound. Loosen the tourniquet every fifteen minutes. **Do not cut X's above the wound.** That often causes more tissue damage than the bite itself and is not known to be effective. If your dog is in pain or is frantic, muzzle him. Call your vet immediately so that he can be getting some anti-venom.

Besides the pain of a bee sting, many dogs are allergic. Allergic dogs will immediately start to swell at the site of the bite. Call your vet immediately. He or she may recommend you give the dog an antihistamine such as Benadryl and if so, will give guidance about the dosage.

BLEEDING

Muzzle your dog if he is in pain. Place a gauze pad or, if one is not available, a clean cloth over the wound and apply pressure. If the wound requires stitches or if the bleeding doesn't stop, call your vet. If the wound is on a leg and continues to bleed, apply a tourniquet but make sure it is loosened every fifteen minutes. If you use a tourniquet or the wound continues bleeding, get to your vet as soon as possible.

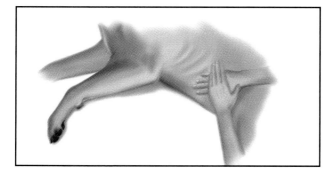

Applying abdominal thrusts can save a choking dog.

CHOKING

If your Australian Shepherd is pawing at his mouth, gagging, coughing or drooling, he may have something caught in his mouth or throat. Open his jaws and shine a flashlight down the throat. If you can see the object, reach in and pull it out, using your fingers, tweezers or a pair of pliers. If you cannot see anything and your dog is still choking, hit the dog behind the neck, between the shoulders to try and dislodge the object. If this fails, use an adapted Heimlich maneuver. Grasp either side of the dog's ribcage and squeeze. Don't break ribs, but try to make a sharp enough movement to cause the air in the lungs to force the object out.

83

If your dog can breathe around the object, get to the vet as soon as possible. If he cannot breathe around the object, you don't have time to move the dog. Keep working on getting the object out.

FRACTURES

Because your Australian Shepherd will be in great pain if he has broken a bone, you should muzzle him immediately. Do not try to set the fracture, but try to immobilize the limb using a piece of wood and then wrapping it with gauze or soft cloth. If there is a door or board you can use as a stretcher to keep the injured limb stable, do it. Transport the dog to the vet as soon as possible.

Make a temporary splint by wrapping the leg in firm casing, then bandaging it.

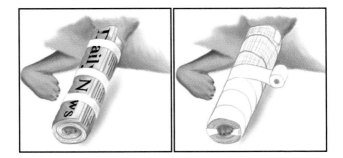

BROKEN NAILS

A ripped or broken toenail can be very painful. If the dog is frantic, muzzle him to protect yourself. If a piece of the nail is hanging, trim it off. Run hydrogen peroxide over the nail. If the nail is bleeding, run it over a soft bar of soap. The soap will help the blood clot. If the quick is showing or if the nail has broken off under the skin, call your veterinarian. Antibiotics might be needed to prevent an infection.

OVERHEATING OR HEATSTROKE

Heatstroke is characterized by rapid or difficult breathing, vomiting, even collapse. You need to act at once; this can be life-threatening. Immediately place your Australian Shepherd in a tub of cold water or, if a tub is not available, run water from a hose over your dog. Use a rectal thermometer to take the dog's temperature and call your vet immediately. Encourage your dog to drink some cool water. Transport the dog to the vet as soon as you can, or as soon as the vet recommends it.

POISONING

Symptoms of poisoning include retching and vomiting, diarrhea, salivation, labored breathing, dilated pupils, weakness, collapse or convulsions. Sometimes one or more symptoms will appear, depending upon the poison. If you suspect your dog has been in contact with a poison, time is critical. Call your veterinarian right away. If your vet is not immediately available, call the Animal Poison Hotline at 1-800-548-2423. The hotline and your vet can better treat your dog if you can tell them what was ingested and approximately how much. **Do not make your dog vomit unless instructed to do so.**

Some of the many household substances harmful to your dog.

Giving Medication

There are two very important things to emphasize about medicating and treating your Australian Shepherd. First of all, if your veterinarian prescribes a treatment, don't be afraid to ask questions. Ask what the drug is, what it does and how long your dog should take it. Ask if there are any side effects you should watch for. Make sure you understand what your dog's problem is, what the course of treatment will do and what you should (or should not) expect.

Second, make sure you follow through on the course of treatment. If your veterinarian said to give the medication for ten days, give it for ten days. Don't stop at five days just because your dog looks better. Again, if you have any problems or reservations, call your vet.

At some time during your Australian Shepherd's life, you will need to give him medication of some kind. Some medications are easy to give, others are difficult. Along the same lines, some dogs are easy to medicate, others can be very difficult.

To put **eye ointment** in the eye without poking the dog with the tube, stand behind your dog and cuddle his head up against your legs. With one hand, gently pull the lower eyelid away from eye just slightly. At the same time, squeeze some of the ointment into the lower eyelid. When the dog closes his eye, the medication will be distributed over the eye.

Squeeze eye ointment into the lower lid.

There are a couple of different ways to give your dog a **pill.** The easiest way is to hide the pill in a piece of cheese or hot dog. Most dogs will just gulp it down. However, some dogs are very clever and will eat the hot dog and spit out the pill. For those dogs, have the dog sit while you stand behind him, straddling the dog's back. Pull the dog's head up and back so the dog's muzzle is pointing up. Open the dog's mouth and very quickly, drop the pill in the back of the throat. Close the dog's mouth and massage his throat until you see the dog swallow. Then, before you let the dog go, open his mouth again and look to make sure he has swallowed the pill.

To give a pill, open the mouth wide, then drop it in the back of the throat.

Liquid medication can be poured into the dog's mouth. However, you must take care that the dog doesn't inhale the medication instead of swallow it. An easier way for many people to give liquids is to measure the amount of medication needed into a turkey baster or a large eyedropper. Have the dog sit and then put the tip of the baster into the dog's mouth from the side, between the molars and the cheek. Holding the dog's mouth shut, squeeze the medication into the dog's mouth while you tilt the dog's head backwards slightly so the medication runs into the mouth instead of out.

Applying **skin ointments** is usually very easy; you simply rub them into the skin according to directions. Keeping your Australian Shepherd from licking the ointments off can be more difficult. With some medications or problems it might not make any difference, but in many cases licking will only make the problem worse. A commercially available product called Bitter Apple is very effective for discouraging some dogs as it has a nasty flavor. Bitter Apple is applied around, not on, the wound, as it contains alcohol. If you need to apply skin medication and your dog is licking, call your veterinarian and ask if you can use Bitter Apple.

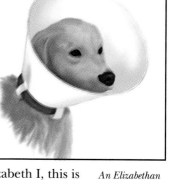

If your dog has a bad skin condition that licking will make worse, or if your dog has stitches, your veterinarian might recommend that you put an **Elizabethan collar** on your dog. Named for the fashion styles of the reign of Queen Elizabeth I, this is a large plastic collar that extends at least to the tip of your dog's nose. It looks like your dog is wearing a huge bucket on his head. The collar is ugly and clumsy, and most dogs absolutely hate it. However, it can prevent your dog from reaching stitches or wounds, giving them time to heal.

An Elizabethan collar keeps your dog from licking a fresh wound.

Health Problems in the Australian Shepherd

Autoimmune Problems   The dog's immune system protects him from disease; when a virus or bacteria enters the body, white blood cells are triggered to combat them. In a dog with an immune system problem, the body will not produce these white blood cells, or with an autoimmune problem, it will begin producing white blood cells to attack itself. Although the causes of autoimmune disease can vary, some researchers feel that there is a genetic predisposition toward it. Dogs with any autoimmune disease should not be used for breeding.

Bloat Bloat is the acute dilation of the stomach, caused when the stomach fills with gas and air and as a result, swells. This swelling prevents the dog from vomiting or passing gas, and as a result, the pressure builds, cutting off blood from the heart and to other parts of the body. This causes shock or heart failure, both of which can cause death. Bloat can also cause torsion, where the stomach turns on its long axis, again causing death.

The first symptoms of bloat are obvious. The dog will be pacing or panting, showing signs of distress. The dog's sides will begin to distend. To be successful, treatment should begin at once—there is no time to fool around. If the pressure is not immediately relieved, death can follow within an hour.

To prevent bloat, do not allow your Australian Shepherd to drink large quantities of water after exercising or after eating. Feed two smaller meals each day instead of one large meal and limit exercise after eating until a couple hours have passed. Feed a good quality food, preferably one that does not expand significantly when wet and that does not produce large quantities of gas.

To see how much your dog's food expands, or to see how much gas the food produces, take a handful of the kibble and drop it in a bowl of warm water. Let it set. After fifteen minutes, look at the food. Some foods will be wet but will not enlarge. This is good. Other foods will triple their size when wet; this can be dangerous if it happens in your dog's stomach. Some foods

---

WHEN TO CALL THE VET

In any emergency situation, you should call your veterinarian immediately. You can make the difference in your dog's life by staying as calm as possible when you call and by giving the doctor or the assistant as much information as possible before you leave for the clinic. That way, the vet will be able to take immediate, specific action to remedy your dog's situation.

Emergencies include acute abdominal pain, suspected poisoning, snakebite, burns, frostbite, shock, dehydration, abnormal vomiting or bleeding, and deep wounds. You are the best judge of your dog's health, as you live with and observe him every day. Don't hesitate to call your veterinarian if you suspect trouble.

will produce gas bubbles, almost as if they were car-
bonated. Again, this can be bad news in your dog's
stomach.

Cancer Unfortunately, some Australian Shepherd
lineages seem to be prone to cancer. Cancer in dogs,
just as in people, is not one disease but a variety of diseases. Although research is continuing, it is unknown
how or why some cells go on a rampage and become
cancerous.

When you examine your Australian Shepherd each
day, be aware of any lumps or bumps you might feel,
especially as your dog is growing older. Your veterinarian can biopsy any suspicious lump and if it is cancer, it
can often be removed. Early removal has the best
chance of success. Unfortunately, cancer is often fatal.

Eye Defects Unfortunately, Aussies have been
known to have some eye defects. There are several different types of eye defects found. Some are known,
others are still being researched. It is still unknown
how many are genetically transmitted, although most
are assumed to be hereditary. Researchers do know
that the genes that cause eye defects are neither simple
recessive nor dominants. It seems that multiple genes
and modifiers might play a part in different defects.

Aussies should have an eye screening as early as eight
weeks of age, prior to being sold or going to a new
home. Every Aussie, especially those used in a breeding program, should have his eyes examined each year.
The exam should be performed by a veterinary oph-
thalmologist, certified by the American College of
Veterinary Ophthalmologists (ACVO). Any Aussie
showing signs of any eye defect should be removed
from breeding, and serious consideration should be
paid to removing that dog's parents from future breeding, as well as any possible offspring.

Hip Dysplasia Hip Dysplasia (HD) is a disease of the
coxofemoral joint; to put it simply, it is a failure of the
head of the femur (thigh bone) to fit into the acetab-
ulum (hip socket). HD is not simply caused by poorly
formed or positioned bones; many researchers feel

that the muscles and tendons in the leg and hip may also play a part in the disease.

HD is considered to be a polygenic inherited disorder, which means that many factors come into play. Many different genes may lead to the disease, not just one. Also, environmental factors may lead to HD, including nutrition and exercise, although the part that environmental factors play in the disease is highly debated among experts.

HD can cause a wide range of problems, from mild lameness to movement irregularities to crippling pain. Dogs with HD must often limit their activities, may need corrective surgery or may even need to be put to sleep because of the pain.

Contrary to popular belief, HD cannot be diagnosed by watching a dog run or by the way he lays down; HD can be diagnosed accurately only by X ray. Once the X ray is taken, it can be sent to the Orthopedic Foundation of America (OFA), which reads, grades and certifies the X rays of dogs over the age of two years. Sound hips are rated excellent, good or fair and the dog's owner receives a certificate with the rating. A dysplastic dog will be rated as mild, moderate or severe. Any dog that is found to be dysplastic should be removed from any breeding program and spayed or neutered.

Panosteitis This disease causes lameness and pain in young, rapidly growing puppies, usually between the ages of six and fourteen months, although it is occasionally seen in dogs up to eighteen months of age. The lameness usually affects one leg at a time and can sporadically move from one leg to another. Some veterinarians prescribe aspirin to relieve the pain and most suggest the dog be kept quiet.

Thyroid Disease The thyroid gland produces hormones which govern or affect a number of different bodily functions. A dog with a thyroid that is producing less hormones than it should may show symptoms ranging from infertility to dry, dull coat and flaky skin, to running eyes or even difficulty walking. Thyroid problems can be diagnosed with a blood test and medication can usually relieve the symptoms fairly rapidly. In most cases, the dog will have to remain on the medication for life.

As Your Australian Shepherd Grows Older

Australian Shepherds can, on the average, live twelve to fourteen years. However, to live that long, remaining happy and healthy, your Australian Shepherd will need your help. Aging in dogs, as in people, brings some changes and problems. You will see your dog's vision dim, his hearing fade and his joints stiffen. Heart and kidney disease are common in older dogs. Reflexes will not be as sharp as they once were and your dog may be more sensitive to heat and cold. He may also get grouchy and be less tolerant of younger dogs, children and other things that may not be part of his normal routine.

Good nutrition, exercise, and loving care will keep your Aussie in peak condition at every stage of his life.

A PRECIOUS TIME

An old dog that has lived his life with you is a special gift. Your old Australian Shepherd knows your ways, your likes and dislikes and your habits. He almost seems able to read your mind and his greatest joy is simply to be close to you. Your old Australian Shepherd may not be able to do the work he did when he was younger, but he can still be a wonderful companion.

ARTHRITIS

Arthritis is common in old dogs. The joints get stiff, especially when it's chilly. Your Aussie may have trouble jumping or getting up in the morning. Give your old dog something soft to sleep on and keep him warm. Talk to your veterinarian about treatment; there are pain relievers that can help.

NUTRITION

Check your dog's teeth frequently and brush them regularly.

As your dog's activity level slows down, he will need to consume fewer calories and as his body ages, he will need less protein. However, some old dogs have a problem digesting foods, too, and this may show up in poor stools and a dull coat. Several dog food manufacturers offer premium quality foods for senior dogs; these foods are more easily digested by the old dog. A heaping tablespoon of live-culture yogurt will also aid digestion.

TEETH

Your Australian Shepherd may need to have his teeth cleaned professionally and this is something that you cannot procrastinate about. Bacteria that builds up on the teeth, called plaque, can infect the gums, get into the bloodstream and cause infections in other parts of the body, including the kidneys and heart.

EXERCISE

Exercise is still important to your Aussie. Your dog needs the stimulation of walking around and seeing and smelling the world. Tailor the exercise to your dog's abilities and needs. If your dog can still chase a tennis ball, great! However, as your dog ages, a slow walk about the neighborhood might be enough.

HOME REMEDIES

If you use herbal or home remedies yourself, you might want to use some for your dog. Many people recommend vitamin C for dogs with arthritis. Rose hips, also a good source of vitamin C, can be good for digestion. Chamomile tea is calming and good for an upset stomach. Yucca is a natural anti-inflammatory and is wonderful for aches and pains as well as arthritis. For more information, check out your local library for books on herbal medicine.

WHEN IT'S TIME

We have the option to keep our dogs from suffering when they are old, ill and in pain. There will be a time when you will need to decide how you are going to handle it. Some feel the time has come when the dog is no longer enjoying life, when he's incontinent and despondent because he has broken housetraining. Only you can make the decision to spare your companion the humiliation of incontinence, convulsions or the inability to stand up or move around.

If your Australian Shepherd must be helped to his death, your veterinarian can give an injection that is an overdose of anesthetic. Your dog will go to sleep and quietly stop breathing. Be there with your dog. Let your arms hold your old friend and let your dog hear your voice saying how much you love him as he goes to sleep. There will be no fear and the last thing your dog will remember is your love.

GRIEVING

A well-loved dog is an emotional investment of unparalleled returns. Unfortunately, our dogs' lives are entirely too short and we must learn to cope with inevitable loss. Grief is a natural reaction to the loss of a loved one, whether it is a pet, a friend or family member. Grief has no set pattern; its intensity and duration are different for each person and for each loss.

Sometimes the best outlet for grief is a good hard cry. For other people, talking about their pet is good therapy. However, don't allow people to say, "But it was only a dog." These people obviously don't understand. Talk to people who own dogs, preferably other people who have lost an old dog and can sympathize with your feelings.

Ceremonies can be good, too, allowing you to say good-bye to your dog and release some tension. Sprinkling your Australian Shepherd's ashes under a fragrant rose bush or burying your dog under a favorite tree will give you a living monument, a place where you can enjoy nature and recall the wonderful times you shared with your Aussie.

Your Happy, Healthy Pet

Your Dog's Name _____

Name on Your Dog's Pedigree (if your dog has one) _____

_____

Where Your Dog Came From _____

_____

Your Dog's Birthday _____

Your Dog's Veterinarian

    Name   _____

    Address   _____

    Phone Number_____

    Emergency Number_____

Your Dog's Health

    Vaccines

    type _____ date given _____

    type _____ date given _____

    type _____ date given _____

    type _____ date given _____

    Heartworm

    date tested _____ type used_____ start date _____

Your Dog's License Number_____

Groomer's Name and Number _____

Dogsitter/Walker's Name and Number_____

Awards Your Dog Has Won

    Award _____ date earned _____

    Award _____ date earned _____

part three

Enjoying
your
Dog

8

Basic
Training

by Ian Dunbar, Ph.D., MRCVS

Training is the jewel in the crown—the most important aspect of doggy husbandry. There is no more important variable influencing dog behavior and temperament than the dog's education: A well-trained, well-behaved and good-natured puppydog is always a joy to live with, but an untrained and uncivilized dog can be a perpetual nightmare. Moreover, deny the dog an education and she will not have the opportunity to fulfill her own canine potential; neither will she have the ability to communicate effectively with her human companions.

Luckily, modern psychological training methods are easy, efficient, effective and, above all, considerably dog-friendly and user-friendly.

Doggy education is as simple as it is enjoyable. But before you can have a good time play-training with your new dog, you have to learn what to do and how to do it. There is no bigger variable influencing the success of dog training than the *owner's* experience and expertise. *Before you embark on the dog's education, you must first educate yourself.*

Basic Training for Owners

Ideally, basic owner training should begin well *before* you select your dog. Find out all you can about your chosen breed first, then master rudimentary training and handling skills. If you already have your puppy-dog, owner training is a dire emergency—the clock is ticking! Especially for puppies, the first few weeks at home are the most important and influential days in the dog's life. Indeed, the cause of most adolescent and adult problems may be traced back to the initial days the pup explores her new home. This is the time to establish the *status quo*—to teach the puppydog how you would like her to behave and so prevent otherwise quite predictable problems.

In addition to consulting breeders and breed books such as this one (which understandably have a positive breed bias), seek out as many pet owners with your breed as you can find. Good points are obvious. What you want to find out are the breed-specific *problems,* so you can nip them in the bud. In particular, you should talk to owners with *adolescent* dogs and make a list of all anticipated problems. Most important, *test drive* at least half a dozen adolescent and adult dogs of your breed yourself. An 8-week-old puppy is deceptively easy to handle, but she will acquire adult size, speed and strength in just four months, so you should learn now what to prepare for.

Puppy and pet dog training classes offer a convenient venue to locate pet owners and observe dogs in action. For a list of suitable trainers in your area, contact the Association of Pet Dog Trainers (see chapter 13). You may also begin your basic owner training by observing other owners in class. Watch as many classes and test drive as many dogs as possible. Select an upbeat, dog-friendly, people-friendly, fun-and-games, puppydog pet training class to learn the ropes. Also, watch training videos and read training books. You must find out what to do and how to do it *before* you have to do it.

Principles of Training

Most people think training comprises teaching the dog to do things such as sit, speak and roll over, but even a 4-week-old pup knows how to do these things already. Instead, the first step in training involves teaching the dog human words for each dog behavior and activity and for each aspect of the dog's environment. That way you, the owner, can more easily participate in the dog's domestic education by directing her to perform specific actions appropriately, that is, at the right time, in the right place and so on. Training opens communication channels, enabling an educated dog to at least understand her owner's requests.

In addition to teaching a dog *what* we want her to do, it is also necessary to teach her *why* she should do what we ask. Indeed, 95 percent of training revolves around motivating the dog *to want to do* what we want. Dogs often understand what their owners want; they just don't see the point of doing it—especially when the owner's repetitively boring and seemingly senseless instructions are totally at odds with much more pressing and exciting doggy distractions. It is not so much the dog that is being stubborn or dominant; rather, it is the owner who has failed to acknowledge the dog's needs and feelings and to approach training from the dog's point of view.

THE MEANING OF INSTRUCTIONS

The secret to successful training is learning how to use training lures to predict or prompt specific behaviors—to coax the dog to do what you want *when* you want. Any highly valued object (such as a treat or toy) may be used as a lure, which the dog will follow with her eyes and nose. Moving the lure in specific ways entices the dog to move her nose, head and entire body in specific ways. In fact, by learning the art of manipulating various lures, it is possible to teach the dog to assume virtually any body position and perform any action. Once you have control over the expression of the dog's behaviors and can elicit any body position or behavior at will, you can easily teach the dog to perform on request.

Teach your dog words for each activity she needs to know, like down.

Tell your dog what you want her to do, use a lure to entice her to respond correctly, then profusely praise and maybe reward her once she performs the desired action. For example, verbally request "Tina, sit!" while you move a squeaky toy upwards and backwards over the dog's muzzle (lure-movement and hand signal), smile knowingly as she looks up (to follow the lure) and sits down (as a result of canine anatomical engineering), then praise her to distraction ("Gooood Tina!"). Squeak the toy, offer a training treat and give your dog and yourself a pat on the back.

Being able to elicit desired responses over and over enables the owner to reward the dog over and over. Consequently, the dog begins to think training is fun. For example, the more the dog is rewarded for sitting, the more she enjoys sitting. Eventually the dog comes to realize that, whereas most sitting is appreciated, sitting immediately upon request usually prompts especially enthusiastic praise and a slew of high-level rewards. The dog begins to sit on cue much of the time, showing that she is starting to grasp the meaning of the owner's verbal request and hand signal.

WHY COMPLY?

Most dogs enjoy initial lure-reward training and are only too happy to comply with their owners' wishes. Unfortunately, repetitive drilling without appreciative feedback tends to diminish the dog's enthusiasm until she eventually fails to see the point of complying anymore. Moreover, as the dog approaches adolescence she becomes more easily distracted as she develops other interests. Lengthy sessions with repetitive exercises tend to bore and demotivate both parties. If it's not fun, the owner doesn't do it and neither does the dog.

Integrate training into your dog's life: The greater number of training sessions each day and the *shorter* they are, the more willingly compliant your dog will

become. Make sure to have a short (just a few seconds) training interlude before every enjoyable canine activity. For example, ask your dog to sit to greet people, to sit before you throw her Frisbee and to sit for her supper. Really, sitting is no different from a canine "Please."

To train your dog, you need gentle hands, a loving heart and a good attitude.

Also, include numerous short training interludes during every enjoyable canine pastime, for example, when playing with the dog or when she is running in the park. In this fashion, doggy distractions may be effectively converted into rewards for training. Just as all games have rules, fun becomes training . . . and training becomes fun.

Eventually, rewards actually become unnecessary to continue motivating your dog. If trained with consideration and kindness, performing the desired behaviors will become self-rewarding and, in a sense, your dog will motivate herself. Just as it is not necessary to reward a human companion during an enjoyable walk in the park, or following a game of tennis, it is hardly necessary to reward our best friend—the dog— for walking by our side or while playing fetch. Human company during enjoyable activities is reward enough for most dogs.

Even though your dog has become self-motivating, it's still good to praise and pet her a lot and offer rewards once in a while, especially for a good job well done. And if for no other reason, praising and rewarding others is good for the human heart.

PUNISHMENT

Without a doubt, lure-reward training is by far the best way to teach: Entice your dog to do what you want and then reward her for doing so. Unfortunately, a human shortcoming is to take the good for granted and to moan and groan at the bad. Specifically, the dog's many good behaviors are ignored while the owner focuses on punishing the dog for making mistakes. In extreme cases, instruction is *limited* to punishing mistakes made by a trainee dog, child, employee or husband, even though it has been proven punishment training is notoriously inefficient and ineffective and is decidedly unfriendly and combative. It teaches the dog that training is a drag, almost as quickly as it teaches the dog to dislike her trainer. Why treat our best friends like our worst enemies?

Punishment training is also much more laborious and time consuming. Whereas it takes only a finite amount of time to teach a dog what to chew, for example, it takes much, much longer to punish the dog for each and every mistake. Remember, *there is only one right way!* So why not teach that right way from the outset?!

To make matters worse, punishment training causes severe lapses in the dog's reliability. Since it is obviously impossible to punish the dog each and every time she misbehaves, the dog quickly learns to distinguish between those times when she must comply (so as to avoid impending punishment) and those times when she need not comply, because punishment is impossible. Such times include when the dog is off leash and 6 feet away, when the owner is otherwise engaged (talking to a friend, watching television, taking a shower, tending to the baby or chatting on the telephone) or when the dog is left at home alone.

Instances of misbehavior will be numerous when the owner is away, because even when the dog complied in the owner's looming presence, she did so unwillingly. The dog was forced to act against her will, rather than molding her will to want to please. Hence, when the owner is absent, not only does the dog know she need not comply, she simply does not want to. Again, the trainee is not a stubborn vindictive beast, but rather the trainer has failed to teach. Punishment training invariably creates unpredictable Jekyll and Hyde behavior.

Trainer's Tools

Many training books extol the virtues of a vast array of training paraphernalia and electronic and metallic gizmos, most of which are designed for canine restraint, correction and punishment, rather than for actual facilitation of doggy education. In reality, most effective training tools are not found in stores; they come from within ourselves. In addition to a willing dog, all you really need is a functional human brain, gentle hands, a loving heart and a good attitude.

In terms of equipment, all dogs do require a quality buckle collar to sport dog tags and to attach the leash (for safety and to comply with local leash laws). Hollow chew toys (like Kongs or sterilized longbones) and a dog bed or collapsible crate are musts for housetraining. Three additional tools are required:

1. specific lures (training treats and toys) to predict and prompt specific desired behaviors;

2. rewards (praise, affection, training treats and toys) to reinforce for the dog what a lot of fun it all is; and

3. knowledge—how to convert the dog's favorite activities and games (potential distractions to training) into "life-rewards," which may be employed to facilitate training.

The most powerful of these is *knowledge*. Education is the key! Watch training classes, participate in training classes, watch videos, read books, enjoy play-training with your dog and then your dog will say "Please," and your dog will say "Thank you!"

Housetraining

If dogs were left to their own devices, certainly they would chew, dig and bark for entertainment and then no doubt highlight a few areas of their living space with sprinkles of urine, in much the same way we decorate by hanging pictures. Consequently, when we ask a dog to live with us, we must teach her *where* she may dig, *where* she may perform her toilet duties, *what* she may chew and *when* she may bark. After all, when left at home alone for many hours, we cannot expect the dog to amuse herself by completing crosswords or watching the soaps on TV!

Also, it would be decidedly unfair to keep the house rules a secret from the dog, and then get angry and punish the poor critter for inevitably transgressing rules she did not even know existed. Remember: Without adequate education and guidance, the dog will be forced to establish her own rules—doggy rules—and most probably will be at odds with the owner's view of domestic living.

Since most problems develop during the first few days the dog is at home, prospective dog owners must be certain they are quite clear about the principles of housetraining *before* they get a dog. Early misbehaviors quickly become established as the *status quo*—

becoming firmly entrenched as hard-to-break bad habits, which set the precedent for years to come. Make sure to teach your dog good habits right from the start. Good habits are just as hard to break as bad ones!

Ideally, when a new dog comes home, try to arrange for someone to be present as much as possible during the first few days (for adult dogs) or weeks for puppies. With only a little forethought, it is surprisingly easy to find a puppy sitter, such as a retired person, who would be willing to eat from your refrigerator and watch your television while keeping an eye on the newcomer to encourage the dog to play with chew toys and to ensure she goes outside on a regular basis.

POTTY TRAINING

To teach the dog where to relieve herself:

1. never let her make a single mistake;
2. let her know where you want her to go; and
3. handsomely reward her for doing so: "GOOOOOOOD DOG!!!" liver treat, liver treat, liver treat!

Preventing Mistakes

A single mistake is a training disaster, since it heralds many more in future weeks. And each time the dog soils the house, this further reinforces the dog's unfortunate preference for an indoor, carpeted toilet. *Do not let an unhousetrained dog have full run of the house.*

When you are away from home, or cannot pay full attention, confine the dog to an area where elimination is appropriate, such as an outdoor run or, better still, a small, comfortable indoor kennel with access to an outdoor run. When confined in this manner, most dogs will naturally housetrain themselves.

If that's not possible, confine the dog to an area, such as a utility room, kitchen, basement or garage, where elimination may not be desired in the long run but as an interim measure it is certainly preferable to doing it all around the house. Use newspaper to cover the floor of the dog's day room. The newspaper may be used to soak up the urine and to wrap up and dispose of the feces. Once your dog develops a preferred spot for eliminating, it is only necessary to cover that part of the floor with newspaper. The smaller papered area may then be moved (only a little each day) towards the door to the outside. Thus the dog will develop the tendency to go to the door when she needs to relieve herself.

Never confine an unhousetrained dog to a crate for long periods. Doing so would force the dog to soil the crate and ruin its usefulness as an aid for housetraining (see the following discussion).

Teaching Where

In order to teach your dog where you would like her to do her business, you have to be there to direct the proceedings—an obvious, yet often neglected, fact of life. In order to be there to teach the dog *where* to go, you need to know *when* she needs to go. Indeed, the success of housetraining depends on the owner's ability to predict these times. Certainly, a regular feeding schedule will facilitate prediction somewhat, but there is nothing like "loading the deck" and influencing the timing of the outcome yourself!

Whenever you are at home, make sure the dog is under constant supervision and/or confined to a small

The first few weeks at home are the most important and influential in your dog's life.

area. If already well trained, simply instruct the dog to lie down in her bed or basket. Alternatively, confine the dog to a crate (doggy den) or tie-down (a short, 18-inch lead that can be clipped to an eye hook in the baseboard near her bed). Short-term close confinement strongly inhibits urination and defecation, since the dog does not want to soil her sleeping area. Thus, when you release the puppydog each hour, she will definitely need to urinate immediately and defecate every third or fourth hour. Keep the dog confined to her doggy den and take her to her intended toilet area each hour, every hour and on the hour.

When taking your dog outside, instruct her to sit quietly before opening the door—she will soon learn to sit by the door when she needs to go out!

Teaching Why

Being able to predict when the dog needs to go enables the owner to be on the spot to praise and reward the dog. Each hour, hurry the dog to the intended toilet area in the yard, issue the appropriate instruction ("Go pee!" or "Go poop!"), then give the dog three to four minutes to produce. Praise and offer a couple of training treats when successful. The treats are important because many people fail to praise their dogs with feeling . . . and housetraining is hardly the time for understatement. So either loosen up and enthusiastically praise that dog: "Wuzzzer-wuzzer-wuzzer, hoooser good wuffer den? Hoooo went pee for Daddy?" Or say "Good dog!" as best you can and offer the treats for effect.

Following elimination is an ideal time for a spot of play-training in the yard or house. Also, an empty dog may be allowed greater freedom around the house for the next half hour or so, just as long as you keep an eye out to make sure she does not get into other kinds of mischief. If you are preoccupied and cannot pay full attention, confine the dog to her doggy den once more to enjoy a peaceful snooze or to play with her many chew toys.

If your dog does not eliminate within the allotted time outside—no biggie! Back to her doggy den, and then try again after another hour.

As I own large dogs, I always feel more relaxed walking an empty dog, knowing that I will not need to finish our stroll weighted down with bags of feces!

Beware of falling into the trap of walking the dog to get her to eliminate. The good ol' dog walk is such an enormous highlight in the dog's life that it represents the single biggest potential reward in domestic dogdom. However, when in a hurry, or during inclement weather, many owners abruptly terminate the walk the moment the dog has done her business. This, in effect, severely punishes the dog for doing the right thing, in the right place at the right time. Consequently, many dogs become strongly inhibited from eliminating outdoors because they know it will signal an abrupt end to an otherwise thoroughly enjoyable walk.

Instead, instruct the dog to relieve herself in the yard prior to going for a walk. If you follow the above instructions, most dogs soon learn to eliminate on cue. As soon as the dog eliminates, praise (and offer a treat or two)—"Good dog! Let's go walkies!" Use the walk as a reward for eliminating in the yard. If the dog does not go, put her back in her doggy den and think about a walk later on. You will find with a "No feces—no walk" policy, your dog will become one of the fastest defecators in the business.

If you do not have a backyard, instruct the dog to eliminate right outside your front door prior to the walk. Not only will this facilitate clean up and disposal of the feces in your own trash can but, also, the walk may again be used as a colossal reward.

CHEWING AND BARKING

Short-term close confinement also teaches the dog that occasional quiet moments are a reality of domestic living. Your puppydog is extremely impressionable during her first few weeks at home. Regular confinement at this time soon exerts a calming influence over the dog's personality. Remember, once the dog is housetrained and calmer, there will be a whole lifetime ahead for the dog to enjoy full run of the house and garden. On the other hand, by letting the newcomer have unrestricted access to the entire household and allowing her to run willy-nilly, she will most certainly develop a bunch of behavior problems in short order, no doubt necessitating confinement later in life. It would not be fair to remedially restrain and confine a dog you have trained, through neglect, to run free.

When confining the dog, make sure she always has an impressive array of suitable chew toys. Kongs and sterilized longbones (both readily available from pet stores) make the best chew toys, since they are hollow and may be stuffed with treats to heighten the dog's interest. For example, by stuffing the little hole at the top of a Kong with a small piece of freeze-dried liver, the dog will not want to leave it alone.

Remember, treats do not have to be junk food and they certainly should not represent extra calories. Rather, treats should be part of each dog's regular

daily diet: Some food may be served in the dog's bowl for breakfast and dinner, some food may be used as training treats, and some food may be used for stuffing chew toys. I regularly stuff my dogs' many Kongs with different shaped biscuits and kibble.

Make sure your puppy has suitable chew toys.

The kibble seems to fall out fairly easily, as do the oval-shaped biscuits, thus rewarding the dog instantaneously for checking out the chew toys. The bone-shaped biscuits fall out after a while, rewarding the dog for worrying at the chew toy. But the triangular biscuits never come out. They remain inside the Kong as lures, maintaining the dog's fascination with her chew toy. To further focus the dog's interest, I always make sure to flavor the triangular biscuits by rubbing them with a little cheese or freeze-dried liver.

To teach come, call your dog, open your arms as a welcoming signal, wave a toy or a treat and praise for every step in your direction.

If stuffed chew toys are reserved especially for times the dog is confined, the puppydog will soon learn to enjoy quiet moments in her doggy den and she will quickly develop a chew-toy habit— a good habit! This is a simple *autoshaping* process; all the owner has to do is set up the situation and the dog all but trains herself— easy and effective. Even when the dog is given run of the house, her first inclination will be to indulge her rewarding chew-toy habit rather than destroy less-attractive household articles, such as curtains, carpets, chairs and compact disks. Similarly, a chew-toy chewer will be less inclined to scratch and chew herself excessively. Also, if the dog busies herself as a recreational chewer, she will be less inclined to develop into a recreational barker or digger when left at home alone.

Stuff a number of chew toys whenever the dog is left confined and remove the extra-special-tasting treats when you return. Your dog will now amuse herself with her chew toys before falling asleep and then resume playing with her chew toys when she expects you to return. Since most owner-absent misbehavior happens right after you leave and right before your expected return, your puppydog will now be conveniently preoccupied with her chew toys at these times.

Come and Sit

Most puppies will happily approach virtually anyone, whether called or not; that is, until they collide with adolescence and develop other more important doggy interests, such as sniffing a multiplicity of exquisite odors on the grass. Your mission, Mr./Ms. Owner, is to teach and reward the pup for coming reliably, willingly and happily when called—and you have just three months to get it done. Unless adequately reinforced, your puppy's tendency to approach people will self-destruct by adolescence.

Call your dog ("Tina, come!"), open your arms (and maybe squat down) as a welcoming signal, waggle a treat or toy as a lure and reward the puppydog when she comes running. Do not wait to praise the dog until she reaches you—she may come 95 percent of the way and then run off after some distraction. Instead, praise the dog's *first* step towards you and continue praising enthusiastically for *every* step she takes in your direction.

When the rapidly approaching puppy dog is three lengths away from impact, instruct her to sit ("Tina, sit!") and hold the lure in front of you in an outstretched hand to prevent her from hitting you midchest and knocking you flat on your back! As Tina decelerates to nose the lure, move the treat upwards and backwards just over her muzzle with an upwards motion of your extended arm (palm-upwards). As the dog looks up to follow the lure, she will sit down (if she jumps up, you are holding the lure too high). Praise the dog for sitting. Move backwards and call her again. Repeat this many times over, always praising when Tina comes and sits; on occasion, reward her.

For the first couple of trials, use a training treat both as a lure to entice the dog to come and sit and as a reward for doing so. Thereafter, try to use different items as lures and rewards. For example, lure the dog with a Kong or Frisbee but reward her with a food treat. Or lure the dog with a food treat but pat her and throw a tennis ball as a reward. After just a few repetitions, dispense with the lures and rewards; the dog will begin to respond willingly to your verbal requests and hand signals just for the prospect of praise from your heart and affection from your hands.

Instruct every family member, friend and visitor how to get the dog to come and sit. Invite people over for a series of pooch parties; do not keep the pup a secret— let other people enjoy this puppy, and let the pup enjoy other people. Puppydog parties are not only fun, they easily attract a lot of people to help *you* train *your* dog. Unless you teach your dog how to meet people, that is, to sit for greetings, no doubt the dog will resort to jumping up. Then you and the visitors will get annoyed, and the dog will be punished. This is not fair. *Send out those invitations for puppy parties and teach your dog to be mannerly and socially acceptable.*

Even though your dog quickly masters obedient recalls in the house, her reliability may falter when playing in the backyard or local park. Ironically, it is *the owner* who has unintentionally trained the dog *not* to respond in these instances. By allowing the dog to play and run around and otherwise have a good time, but then to call the dog to put her on leash to take her home, the dog quickly learns playing is fun but training is a drag. Thus, playing in the park becomes a severe distraction, which works against training. Bad news!

Instead, whether playing with the dog off leash or on leash, request her to come at frequent intervals—say, every minute or so. On most occasions, praise and pet the dog for a few seconds while she is sitting, then tell her to go play again. For especially fast recalls, offer a couple of training treats and take the time to praise and pet the dog enthusiastically before releasing her. The dog will learn that coming when called is not necessarily the end of the play session, and neither is it the end of the world; rather, it signals an enjoyable, quality time-out with the owner before resuming play once more. In fact, playing in the park now becomes a very effective life-reward, which works to facilitate training by reinforcing each obedient and timely recall. Good news!

Sit, Down, Stand and Rollover

Teaching the dog a variety of body positions is easy for owner and dog, impressive for spectators and extremely useful for all. Using lure-reward techniques, it is possible to train several positions at once to verbal commands or hand signals (which impress the socks off onlookers).

Sit and ***down***—the two control commands—prevent or resolve nearly a hundred behavior problems. For example, if the dog happily and obediently sits or lies down when requested, she cannot jump on visitors, dash out the front door, run around and chase her tail, pester other dogs, harass cats or annoy family, friends or strangers. Additionally, "Sit" or "Down" are the best emergency commands for off-leash control.

It is easier to teach and maintain a reliable sit than maintain a reliable recall. *Sit* is the purest and simplest of commands—either the dog is sitting or she is not. If there is any change of circumstances or potential danger in the park, for example, simply instruct the dog to sit. If she sits, you have a number of options: Allow the dog to resume playing when she is safe, walk up and put the dog on leash or call the dog. The dog will be much more likely to come when called if she has already acknowledged her compliance by sitting. If the dog does not sit in the park—train her to!

Stand and ***rollover-stay*** are the two positions for examining the dog. Your veterinarian will love you to distraction if you take a little time to teach the dog to stand still and roll over and play possum. Also, your vet bills will be smaller because it will take the veterinarian less time to examine your dog. The rollover-stay is an especially useful command and is really just a variation of the down-stay: Whereas the dog lies prone in the traditional down, she lies supine in the rollover-stay.

As with teaching come and sit, the training techniques to teach the dog to assume all other body positions on cue are user-friendly and dog-friendly. Simply give the appropriate request, lure the dog into the desired body position using a training treat or toy and then *praise* (and maybe reward) the dog as soon as she complies. Try not to touch the dog to get her to respond. If you teach the dog by guiding her into position, the dog will quickly learn that rump-pressure means sit, for example, but as yet you still have no control over your dog if she is just 6 feet away. It will still be necessary to teach the dog to sit on request. So do not make training a time-consuming two-step process; instead, teach the dog to sit to a verbal request or hand signal from the outset. Once the dog sits willingly when requested, by all means use your hands to pet the dog when she does so.

To teach *down* when the dog is already sitting, say "Tina, down!," hold the lure in one hand (palm down) and lower that hand to the floor between the dog's forepaws. As the dog lowers her head to follow the lure, slowly move the lure away from the dog just a fraction (in front of her paws). The dog will lie down as she stretches her nose forward to follow the lure. Praise the dog when she does so. If the dog stands up, you pulled the lure away too far and too quickly.

When teaching the dog to lie down from the standing position, say "Down" and lower the lure to the floor as before. Once the dog has lowered her forequarters and assumed a play bow, gently and slowly move the lure *towards* the dog between her forelegs. Praise the dog as soon as her rear end plops down.

After just a couple of trials it will be possible to alternate sits and downs and have the dog energetically perform doggy push-ups. Praise the dog a lot, and after half a dozen or so push-ups reward the dog with a training treat or toy. You will notice the more energetically you move your arm—upwards (palm up) to get the dog to sit, and downwards (palm down) to get the dog to lie down—the more energetically the dog responds to your requests. Now try training the dog in silence and you will notice she has also learned to respond to hand signals. Yeah! Not too shabby for the first session.

To teach *stand* from the sitting position, say "Tina, stand," slowly move the lure half a dog-length away from the dog's nose, keeping it at nose level, and praise the dog as she stands to follow the lure. As soon

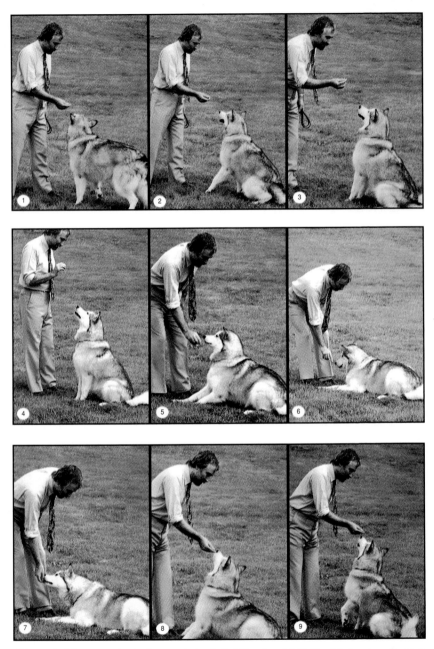

Using a food lure to teach sit, down and stand. 1) "Phoenix, sit." 2) Hand palm upwards, move lure up and back over dog's muzzle. 3) "Good sit, Phoenix!" 4) "Phoenix, down." 5) Hand palm downwards, move lure down to lie between dog's forepaws. 6) "Phoenix, off. Good down, Phoenix!" 7) "Phoenix, sit!" 8) Palm upwards, move lure up and back, keeping it close to dog's muzzle. 9) "Good sit, Phoenix!"

10) *"Phoenix, stand!"* 11) *Move lure away from dog at nose height, then lower it a tad.* 12) *"Phoenix, off! Good stand, Phoenix!"* 13) *"Phoenix, down!"* 14) *Hand palm downwards, move lure down to lie between dog's forepaws.* 15) *"Phoenix, off! Good down-stay, Phoenix!"* 16) *"Phoenix, stand!"* 17) *Move lure away from dog's muzzle up to nose height.* 18) *"Phoenix, off! Good stand-stay, Phoenix. Now we'll make the vet and groomer happy!"*

as the dog stands, lower the lure to just beneath the dog's chin to entice her to look down; otherwise she will stand and then sit immediately. To prompt the dog to stand from the down position, move the lure half a dog-length upwards and away from the dog, holding the lure at standing nose height from the floor.

Teaching **rollover** is best started from the down position, with the dog lying on one side, or at least with both hind legs stretched out on the same side. Say "Tina, bang!" and move the lure backwards and alongside the dog's muzzle to her elbow (on the side of her outstretched hind legs). Once the dog looks to the side and backwards, very slowly move the lure upwards to the dog's shoulder and backbone. Tickling the dog in the goolies (groin area) often invokes a reflex-raising of the hind leg as an appeasement gesture, which facilitates the tendency to roll over. If you move the lure too quickly and the dog jumps into the standing position, have patience and start again. As soon as the dog rolls onto her back, keep the lure stationary and mesmerize the dog with a relaxing tummy rub.

To teach **rollover-stay** when the dog is standing or moving, say "Tina, bang!" and give the appropriate hand signal (with index finger pointed and thumb cocked in true Sam Spade fashion), then in one fluid movement lure her to first lie down and then rollover-stay as above.

Teaching the dog to **stay** in each of the above four positions becomes a piece of cake after first teaching the dog not to worry at the toy or treat training lure. This is best accomplished by hand feeding dinner kibble. Hold a piece of kibble firmly in your hand and softly instruct "Off!" Ignore any licking and slobbering *for however long the dog worries at the treat*, but say "Take it!" and offer the kibble *the instant* the dog breaks contact with her muzzle. Repeat this a few times, and then up the ante and insist the dog remove her muzzle for one whole second before offering the kibble. Then progressively refine your criteria and have the dog not touch your hand (or treat) for longer and longer periods on each trial, such as for two seconds, four seconds, then six, ten, fifteen, twenty, thirty seconds and so on.

The dog soon learns: (1) worrying at the treat never gets results, whereas (2) noncontact is often rewarded after a variable time lapse.

Teaching *"Off!"* has many useful applications in its own right. Additionally, instructing the dog not to touch a training lure often produces spontaneous and magical stays. Request the dog to stand-stay, for example, and not to touch the lure. At first set your sights on a short two-second stay before rewarding the dog. (Remember, every long journey begins with a single step.) However, on subsequent trials, gradually and progressively increase the length of stay required to receive a reward. In no time at all your dog will stand calmly for a minute or so.

Relevancy Training

Once you have taught the dog what you expect her to do when requested to come, sit, lie down, stand, roll-over and stay, the time is right to teach the dog *why* she should comply with your wishes. The secret is to have many (*many*) extremely short training interludes (two to five seconds each) at numerous (*numerous*) times during the course of the dog's day. Especially work with the dog immediately *before* the dog's good times and *during* the dog's good times. For example, ask your dog to sit and/or lie down each time before opening doors, serving meals, offering treats and tummy rubs; ask the dog to perform a few controlled doggy push-ups before letting her off leash or throwing a tennis ball; and perhaps request the dog to sit-down-sit-stand-down-stand-rollover before inviting her to cuddle on the couch.

Similarly, request the dog to sit many times during play or on walks, and in no time at all the dog will be only too pleased to follow your instructions because she has learned that a compliant response heralds all sorts of goodies. Basically all you are trying to teach the dog is how to say please: "Please throw the tennis ball. Please may I snuggle on the couch."

Remember, it is important to keep training interludes short and to have many short sessions each and every day. The shortest (and most useful) session comprises asking the dog to sit and then go play during a play session. When trained this way, your dog will soon associate training with good times. In fact, the dog may be unable to distinguish between training and good times and, indeed, there should be no distinction. The warped concept that training involves forcing the dog to comply and/or dominating her will is totally at odds with the picture of a truly well-trained dog. In reality, enjoying a game of training with a dog is no different from enjoying a game of backgammon or tennis with a friend; and walking with a dog should be no different from strolling with a spouse, or with buddies on the golf course.

Walk by Your Side

Many people attempt to teach a dog to heel by putting her on a leash and physically correcting the dog when she makes mistakes. There are a number of things seriously wrong with this approach, the first being that most people do not want precision heeling; rather, they simply want the dog to follow or walk by their side. Second, when physically restrained during "training," even though the dog may grudgingly mope by your side when "handcuffed" on leash, let's see what happens when she is off leash. History! The dog is in the next county because she never enjoyed walking with you on leash and you have no control over her off leash. So let's just teach the dog off leash from the outset to *want* to walk with us. Third, if the dog has not been trained to heel, it is a trifle hasty to think about punishing the poor dog for making mistakes and breaking heeling rules she didn't even know existed. This is simply not fair! Surely, if the dog had been adequately taught how to heel, she would seldom make mistakes and hence there would be no need to correct the dog. Remember, each mistake and each correction (punishment) advertise the trainer's inadequacy, not the dog's. The dog is not stubborn, she is not stupid and she is not bad. Even if she were, she would still require training, so let's train her properly.

Let's teach the dog to *enjoy* following us and to *want* to walk by our side off leash. Then it will be easier to teach high-precision off-leash heeling patterns if desired. Before going on outdoor walks, it is necessary to teach the dog not to pull. Then it becomes easy to teach on-leash walking and heeling because the dog already wants to walk with you, she is familiar with the desired walking and heeling positions and she knows not to pull.

FOLLOWING

Start by training your dog to follow you. Many puppies will follow if you simply walk away from them and maybe click your fingers or chuckle. Adult dogs may require additional enticement to stimulate them to follow, such as a training lure or, at the very least, a lively trainer. To teach the dog to follow: (1) keep walking and (2) walk away from the dog. If the dog attempts to lead or lag, change pace; slow down if the dog forges too far ahead, but speed up if she lags too far behind. Say "Steady!" or "Easy!" each time before you slow down and "Quickly!" or "Hustle!" each time before you speed up, and the dog will learn to change pace on cue. If the dog lags or leads too far, or if she wanders right or left, simply walk quickly in the opposite direction and maybe even run away from the dog and hide.

Practicing is a lot of fun; you can set up a course in your home, yard or park to do this. Indoors, entice the dog to follow upstairs, into a bedroom, into the bathroom, downstairs, around the living room couch, zigzagging between dining room chairs and into the kitchen for dinner. Outdoors, get the dog to follow around park benches, trees, shrubs and along walkways and lines in the grass. (For safety outdoors, it is advisable to attach a long line on the dog, but never exert corrective tension on the line.)

121

Enjoying Your
Dog

Remember, following has a lot to do with attitude—
your attitude! Most probably your dog will *not* want to
follow Mr. Grumpy Troll with the personality of wilted
lettuce. Lighten up—walk with a jaunty step, whistle a
happy tune, sing, skip and tell jokes to your dog and
she will be right there by your side.

BY YOUR SIDE

It is smart to train the dog to walk close on one side or
the other—either side will do, your choice. When walking, jogging or cycling, it is generally bad news to have
the dog suddenly cut in front of you. In fact, I train my
dogs to walk "By my side" and "Other side"—both very
useful instructions. It is possible to position the dog
fairly accurately by looking to the appropriate side and
clicking your fingers or slapping your thigh on that
side. A precise positioning may be attained by holding
a training lure, such as a chew toy, tennis ball or food
treat. Stop and stand still several times throughout the
walk, just as you would when window shopping or
meeting a friend. Use the lure to make sure the dog
slows down and stays close whenever you stop.

When teaching the dog to heel, we generally want
her to sit in heel position when we stop. Teach heel

Using a toy to teach sit-heel-sit sequences: 1) "Phoenix, sit!" Standing still, move lure up and back over dog's muzzle . . . 2) to position dog sitting in heel position on your left side. 3) Say "Phoenix, heel!" and walk ahead, wagging lure in left hand. Change lure to right hand in preparation for sit signal. Say "Sit" and then . . .

position at the standstill and the dog will learn that the default heel position is sitting by your side (left or right—your choice, unless you wish to compete in obedience trials, in which case the dog must heel on the left).

Several times a day, stand up and call your dog to come and sit in heel position—"Tina, heel!" For example, instruct the dog to come to heel each time there are commercials on TV, or each time you turn a page of a novel, and the dog will get it in a single evening.

Practice straight-line heeling and turns separately. With the dog sitting at heel, teach her to turn in place. After each quarter-turn, half-turn or full turn in place, lure the dog to sit at heel. Now it's time for short straight-line heeling sequences, no more than a few steps at a time. Always think of heeling in terms of sit-heel-sit sequences—start and end with the dog in position and do your best to keep her there when moving. Progressively increase the number of steps in each sequence. When the dog remains close for 20 yards of straight-line heeling, it is time to add a few turns and then sign up for a happy-heeling obedience class to get some advice from the experts.

4) use hand signal to lure dog to sit as you stop. Eventually, dog will sit automatically at heel whenever you stop. 5) "Good dog!"

No Pulling on Leash

You can start teaching your dog not to pull on leash anywhere—in front of the television or outdoors—but regardless of location, you must not take a single step with tension in the leash. For a reason known only to dogs, even just a couple of paces of pulling on leash is intrinsically motivating and diabolically rewarding. Instead, attach the leash to the dog's collar, grasp the other end firmly with both hands held close to your chest, and stand still—do not budge an inch. Have somebody watch you with a stopwatch to time your progress, or else you will never believe this will work and so you will not even try the exercise, and your shoulder and the dog's neck will be traumatized for years to come.

Stand still and wait for the dog to stop pulling, and to sit and/or lie down. All dogs stop pulling and sit eventually. Most take only a couple of minutes; the all-time record is $22\frac{1}{2}$ minutes. Time how long it takes. Gently praise the dog when she stops pulling, and as soon as she sits, enthusiastically praise the dog and take just one step forward, then immediately stand still. This single step usually demonstrates the ballistic reinforcing nature of pulling on leash; most dogs explode to the end of the leash, so be prepared for the strain. Stand firm and wait for the dog to sit again. Repeat this half a dozen times and you will probably notice a progressive reduction in the force of the dog's one-step explosions and a radical reduction in the time it takes for the dog to sit each time.

As the dog learns "Sit we go" and "Pull we stop," she will begin to walk forward calmly with each single step and automatically sit when you stop. Now try two steps before you stop. Wooooooo! Scary! When the dog has mastered two steps at a time, try for three. After each success, progressively increase the number of steps in the sequence: try four steps and then six, eight, ten and twenty steps before stopping. Congratulations! You are now walking the dog on leash.

Whenever walking with the dog (off leash or on leash), make sure you stop periodically to practice a few position commands and stays before instructing the dog to "Walk on!" (Remember, you want the dog to be compliant everywhere, not just in the kitchen when her dinner is at hand.) For example, stopping every 25 yards to briefly train the dog amounts to over 200 training interludes within a single 3-mile stroll. And each training session is in a different location. You will not believe the improvement within just the first mile of the first walk.

To put it another way, integrating training into a walk offers 200 separate opportunities to use the continuance of the walk as a reward to reinforce the dog's education. Moreover, some training interludes may comprise continuing education for the dog's walking skills: Alternate short periods of the dog walking calmly by your side with periods when the dog is allowed to sniff and investigate the environment. Now sniffing odors on the grass and meeting other dogs become rewards which reinforce the dog's calm and mannerly demeanor. Good Lord! Whatever next? Many enjoyable walks together of course. Happy trails!

THE IMPORTANCE OF TRICKS

Nothing will improve a dog's quality of life better than having a few tricks under her belt. Teaching any trick expands the dog's vocabulary, which facilitates communication and improves the owner's control. Also, specific tricks help prevent and resolve specific behavior problems. For example, by teaching the dog to fetch her toys, the dog learns carrying a toy makes the owner happy and, therefore, will be more likely to chew her toy than other inappropriate items.

More important, teaching tricks prompts owners to lighten up and train with a sunny disposition. Really, tricks should be no different from any other behaviors we put on cue. But they are. When teaching tricks, owners have a much sweeter attitude, which in turn motivates the dog and improves her willingness to comply. The dog feels tricks are a blast, but formal commands are a drag. In fact, tricks are so enjoyable, they may be used as rewards in training by asking the dog to come, sit and down-stay and then rollover for a tummy rub. Go on, try it: Crack a smile and even giggle when the dog promptly and willingly lies down and stays.

Most important, performing tricks prompts onlookers to smile and giggle. Many people are scared of dogs, especially large ones. And nothing can be more off-putting for a dog than to be constantly confronted by strangers who don't like her because of her size or the way she looks. Uneasy people put the dog on edge, causing her to back off and bark, only frightening people all the more. And so a vicious circle develops, with the people's fear fueling the dog's fear *and vice versa*. Instead, tie a pink ribbon to your dog's collar and practice all sorts of tricks on walks and in the park, and you will be pleasantly amazed how it changes people's attitudes toward your friendly dog. The dog's repertoire of tricks is limited only by the trainer's imagination. Below I have described three of my favorites:

SPEAK AND SHUSH

The training sequence involved in teaching a dog to bark on request is no different from that used when training any behavior on cue: request—lure—response—reward. As always, the secret of success lies in finding an effective lure. If the dog always barks at the doorbell, for example, say "Rover, speak!", have an accomplice ring the doorbell, then reward the dog for barking. After a few woofs, ask Rover to "Shush!", waggle a food treat under her nose (to entice her to sniff and thus to shush), praise her when quiet and eventually offer the treat as a reward. Alternate "Speak" and "Shush," progressively increasing the length of shush-time between each barking bout.

PLAY BOW

With the dog standing, say "Bow!" and lower the food lure (palm upwards) to rest between the dog's forepaws. Praise as the dog lowers her forequarters and sternum to the ground (as when teaching the down), but then lure the dog to stand and offer the treat. On successive trials, gradually increase the length of time the dog is required to remain in the play bow posture in order to gain a food reward. If the dog's rear end collapses into a down, say nothing and offer no reward; simply start over.

BE A BEAR

With the dog sitting backed into a corner to prevent her from toppling over backwards, say "Be a bear!" With bent paw and palm down, raise a lure upwards and backwards along the top of the dog's muzzle. Praise the dog when she sits up on her haunches and offer the treat as a reward. To prevent the dog from standing on her hind legs, keep the lure closer to the dog's muzzle. On each trial, progressively increase the length of time the dog is required to sit up to receive a food reward. Since lure-reward training is so easy, teach the dog to stand and walk on her hind legs as well!

Teaching "Be a Bear"

Getting
Active
with your Dog

by Bardi McLennan

Once you and your dog have graduated from basic obedience training and are beginning to work together as a team, you can take part in the growing world of dog activities. There are so many fun things to do with your dog! Just remember, people and dogs don't always learn at the same pace, so don't be upset if you (or your dog) need more than two basic training courses before your team becomes operational. Even smart dogs don't go straight to college from kindergarten!

Just as there are events geared to certain types of dogs, so there are ones that are more appealing to certain types of people. In some activities, you give the commands and your dog does the work (upland game hunting is one example), while in others, such as agility, you'll both get a workout. You may want to aim for prestigious titles to add to your dog's name, or you may want nothing more than the sheer enjoyment of being around other people and their dogs. Passive or active, participation has its own rewards.

Consider your dog's physical capabilities when looking into any of the canine activities. It's easy to see that a Basset Hound is not built for the racetrack, nor would a Chihuahua be the breed of choice for pulling a sled. A loyal dog will attempt almost anything you ask him to do, so it is up to you to know your

All dogs seem to love playing flyball.

dog's limitations. A dog must be physically sound in order to compete at any level in athletic activities, and being mentally sound is a definite plus. Advanced age, however, may not be a deterrent. Many dogs still hunt and herd at ten or twelve years of age. It's entirely possible for dogs to be "fit at 50." Take your dog for a checkup, explain to your vet the type of activity you have in mind and be guided by his or her findings.

You needn't be restricted to breed-specific sports if it's only fun you're after. Certain AKC activities are limited to designated breeds; however, as each new trial, test or sport has grown in popularity, so has the variety of breeds encouraged to participate at a fun level.

But don't shortchange your fun, or that of your dog, by thinking only of the basic function of her breed. Once a dog has learned how to learn, she can be taught to do just about anything as long as the size of the dog is right for the job and you both think it is fun and rewarding. In other words, you are a team.

To get involved in any of the activities detailed in this chapter, look for the names and addresses of the organizations that sponsor them in Chapter 13. You can also ask your breeder or a local dog trainer for contacts.

Official American Kennel Club Activities

The following tests and trials are some of the events sanctioned by the AKC and sponsored by various dog clubs. Your dog's expertise will be rewarded with impressive titles. You can participate just for fun, or be competitive and go for those awards.

OBEDIENCE

Training classes begin with pups as young as three months of age in kindergarten puppy training,

You can compete in obedience trials with a well trained dog.

then advance to pre-novice (all exercises on lead) and go on to novice, which is where you'll start off-lead work. In obedience classes dogs learn to sit, stay, heel and come through a variety of exercises. Once you've got the basics down, you can enter obedience trials and work toward earning your dog's first degree, a C.D. (Companion Dog).

The next level is called "Open," in which jumps and retrieves perk up the dog's interest. Passing grades in competition at this level earn a C.D.X. (Companion Dog Excellent). Beyond that lies the goal of the most ambitious—Utility (U.D. and even U.D.X. or OTCh, an Obedience Champion).

AGILITY

All dogs can participate in the latest canine sport to have gained worldwide popularity for its fun and excitement, agility. It began in England as a canine version of horse show-jumping, but because dogs are more agile and able to perform on verbal commands, extra feats were added such as climbing, balancing and racing through tunnels or in and out of weave poles.

Many of the obstacles (regulation or homemade) can be set up in your own backyard. If the agility bug bites, you could end up in international competition!

For starters, your dog should be obedience trained, even though, in the beginning, the lessons may all be taught on lead. Once the dog understands the commands (and you do, too), it's as easy as guiding the dog over a prescribed course, one obstacle at a time. In competition, the race is against the clock, so wear your running shoes! The dog starts with 200 points and the judge deducts for infractions and misadventures along the way.

All dogs seem to love agility and respond to it as if they were being turned loose in a playground paradise. Your dog's enthusiasm will be contagious; agility turns into great fun for dog and owner.

FIELD TRIALS AND HUNTING TESTS

There are field trials and hunting tests for the sporting breeds—retrievers, spaniels and pointing breeds, and for some hounds—Bassets, Beagles and Dachshunds. Field trials are competitive events that test a dog's ability to perform the functions for which she was bred. Hunting tests, which are open to retrievers,

---

TITLES AWARDED BY THE AKC

Conformation: Ch. (Champion)

Obedience: CD (Companion Dog); CDX (Companion Dog Excellent); UD (Utility Dog); UDX (Utility Dog Excellent); OTCh. (Obedience Trial Champion)

Field: JH (Junior Hunter); SH (Senior Hunter); MH (Master Hunter); AFCh. (Amateur Field Champion); FCh. (Field Champion)

Lure Coursing: JC (Junior Courser); SC (Senior Courser)

Herding: HT (Herding Tested); PT (Pre-Trial Tested); HS (Herding Started); HI (Herding Intermediate); HX (Herding Excellent); HCh. (Herding Champion)

Tracking: TD (Tracking Dog); TDX (Tracking Dog Excellent)

Agility: NAD (Novice Agility); OAD (Open Agility); ADX (Agility Excellent); MAX (Master Agility)

Earthdog Tests: JE (Junior Earthdog); SE (Senior Earthdog); ME (Master Earthdog)

Canine Good Citizen: CGC

Combination: DC (Dual Champion—Ch. and Fch.); TC (Triple Champion—Ch., Fch., and OTCh.)

spaniels and pointing breeds only, are noncompetitive and are a means of judging the dog's ability as well as that of the handler.

Hunting is a very large and complex part of canine sports, and if you own one of the breeds that hunts, the events are a great treat for your dog and you. He gets to do what he was bred for, and you get to work with him and watch him do it. You'll be proud of and amazed at what your dog can do.

Fortunately, the AKC publishes a series of booklets on these events, which outline the rules and regulations and include a glossary of the sometimes complicated terms. The AKC also publishes newsletters for field trialers and hunting test enthusiasts. The United Kennel Club (UKC) also has informative materials for the hunter and his dog.

Retrievers and other sporting breeds get to do what they're bred to in hunting tests.

HERDING TESTS AND TRIALS

Herding, like hunting, dates back to the first known uses man made of dogs. The interest in herding today is widespread, and if you own a herding breed, you can join in the activity. Herding dogs are tested for their natural skills to keep a flock of ducks, sheep or cattle together. If your dog shows potential, you can start at the testing level, where your dog can earn a title for showing an inherent herding ability. With training you can advance to the trial level, where your dog should be capable of controlling even difficult livestock in diverse situations.

LURE COURSING

The AKC Tests and Trials for Lure Coursing are open to traditional sighthounds—Greyhounds, Whippets,

Borzoi, Salukis, Afghan Hounds, Ibizan Hounds and Scottish Deerhounds—as well as to Basenjis and Rhodesian Ridgebacks. Hounds are judged on overall ability, follow, speed, agility and endurance. This is possibly the most exciting of the trials for spectators, because the speed and agility of the dogs is awesome to watch as they chase the lure (or "course") in heats of two or three dogs at a time.

Tracking

Tracking is another activity in which almost any dog can compete because every dog that sniffs the ground when taken outdoors is, in fact, tracking. The hard part comes when the rules as to what, when and where the dog tracks are determined by a person, not the dog! Tracking tests cover a large area of fields, woods and roads. The tracks are laid hours before the dogs go to work on them, and include "tricks" like cross-tracks and sharp turns. If you're interested in search-and-rescue work, this is the place to start.

This tracking dog is hot on the trail.

Earthdog Tests for Small Terriers and Dachshunds

These tests are open to Australian, Bedlington, Border, Cairn, Dandie Dinmont, Smooth and Wire Fox, Lakeland, Norfolk, Norwich, Scottish, Sealyham, Skye, Welsh and West Highland White Terriers as well as Dachshunds. The dogs need no prior training for this terrier sport. There is a qualifying test on the day of the event, so dog and handler learn the rules on the spot. These tests, or "digs," sometimes end with informal races in the late afternoon.

133

Here are some of the extracurricular obedience and racing activities that are not regulated by the AKC or UKC, but are generally run by clubs or a group of dog fanciers and are often open to all.

Canine Freestyle This activity is something new on the scene and is variously likened to dancing, dressage or ice skating. It is meant to show the athleticism of the dog, but also requires showmanship on the part of the dog's handler. If you and your dog like to ham it up for friends, you might want to look into freestyle.

Lure coursing lets sighthounds do what they do best—run!

Scent Hurdle Racing Scent hurdle racing is purely a fun activity sponsored by obedience clubs with members forming competing teams. The height of the hurdles is based on the size of the shortest dog on the team. On a signal, one team dog is released on each of two side-by-side courses and must clear every hurdle before picking up its own dumbbell from a platform and returning over the jumps to the handler. As each dog returns, the next on that team is sent. Of course, that is what the dogs are supposed to do. When the dogs improvise (going under or around the hurdles, stealing another dog's dumbbell, and so forth), it no doubt frustrates the handlers, but just adds to the fun for everyone else.

Flyball This type of racing is similar, but after negotiating the four hurdles, the dog comes to a flyball box, steps on a lever that releases a tennis ball into the air, catches the ball and returns over the hurdles to the starting point. This game also becomes extremely fun for spectators because the dogs sometimes cheat by catching a ball released by the dog in the next lane. Three titles can be earned—Flyball Dog (F.D.), Flyball Dog Excellent (F.D.X.) and Flyball Dog Champion (Fb.D.Ch.)—all awarded by the North American Flyball Association, Inc.

Dogsledding The name conjures up the Rocky Mountains or the frigid North, but you can find dogsled clubs in such unlikely spots as Maryland, North Carolina and Virginia! Dogsledding is primarily for the Nordic breeds such as the Alaskan Malamutes, Siberian Huskies and Samoyeds, but other breeds can try. There are some practical backyard applications to this sport, too. With parental supervision, almost any strong dog could pull a child's sled.

Coming over the A-frame on an agility course.

These are just some of the many recreational ways you can get to know and understand your multifaceted dog better and have fun doing it.

chapter 10

Your Dog
and your
Family

by Bardi McLennan

Adding a dog automatically
increases your family by one, no
matter whether you live alone
in an apartment or are part of a
mother, father and six kids
household. The single-person
family is fair game for numerous and varied canine miscon-
ceptions as to who is dog and
who pays the bills, whereas a
dog in a houseful of children
will consider himself to be just
one of the gang, littermates all.
One dog and one child may
give a dog reason to believe
they are both kids or both dogs.

Either interpretation requires parental supervision and sometimes
speedy intervention.

As soon as one paw goes through the door into your home, Rufus
(or Rufina) has to make many adjustments to become a part of your

family. Your job is to make him fit in as painlessly as possible. An older dog may have some frame of reference from past experience, but to a 10-week-old puppy, everything is brand new: people, furniture, stairs, when and where people eat, sleep or watch TV, his own place and everyone else's space, smells, sounds, outdoors—everything!

Puppies, and newly acquired dogs of any age, do not need what we think of as "freedom." If you leave a new dog or puppy loose in the house, you will almost certainly return to chaotic destruction and the dog will forever after equate your homecoming with a time of punishment to be dreaded. It is unfair to give your dog what amounts to "freedom to get into trouble." Instead, confine him to a crate for brief periods of your absence (up to three or four hours) and, for the long haul, a workday for example, confine him to one untrashable area with his own toys, a bowl of water and a radio left on (low) in another room.

Lots of pets get along with each other just fine.

For the first few days, when not confined, put Rufus on a long leash tied to your wrist or waist. This umbilical cord method enables the dog to learn all about you from your body language and voice, and to learn by his own actions which things in the house are NO! and which ones are rewarded by "Good dog." Housetraining will be easier with the pup always by your side. Speaking of which, accidents do happen. That goal of "completely housetrained" takes up to a year, or the length of time it takes the pup to mature.

The All-Adult Family

Most dogs in an adults-only household today are likely to be latchkey pets, with no one home all day but the dog. When you return after a tough day on the job, the dog can and should be your relaxation therapy. But going home can instead be a daily frustration.

Separation anxiety is a very common problem for the dog in a working household. It may begin with whines and barks of loneliness, but it will soon escalate into a frenzied destruction derby. That is why it is so important to set aside the time to teach a dog to relax when left alone in his confined area and to understand that he can trust you to return.

Let the dog get used to your work schedule in easy stages. Confine him to one room and go in and out of that room over and over again. Be casual about it. No physical, voice or eye contact. When the pup no longer even notices your comings and goings, leave the house for varying lengths of time, returning to stay home for a few minutes and gradually increasing the time away. This training can take days, but the dog is learning that you haven't left him forever and that he can trust you.

Any time you leave the dog, but especially during this training period, be casual about your departure. No anxiety-building fond farewells. Just "Bye" and go! Remember the "Good dog" when you return to find everything more or less as you left it.

If things are a mess (or even a disaster) when you return, greet the dog, take him outside to eliminate, and then put him in his crate while you clean up. Rant and rave in the shower! *Do not* punish the dog. You were not there when it happened, and the rule is: Only punish as you catch the dog in the act of wrongdoing. Obviously, it makes sense to get your latchkey puppy when you'll have a week or two to spend on these training essentials.

Family weekend activities should include Rufus whenever possible. Depending on the pup's age, now is the time for a long walk in the park, playtime in the backyard, a hike in the woods. Socializing is as important as health care, good food and physical exercise, so visiting Aunt Emma or Uncle Harry and the next-door neighbor's dog or cat is essential to developing an out-going, friendly temperament in your pet.

If you are a single adult, socializing Rufus at home and away will prevent him from becoming overly protective of you (or just overly attached) and will also prevent such behavioral problems as dominance or fear of strangers.

Babies

Whether already here or on the way, babies figure larger than life in the eyes of a dog. If the dog is there first, let him in on all your baby preparations in the house. When baby arrives, let Rufus sniff any item of clothing that has been on the baby before Junior comes home. Then let Mom greet the dog first before introducing the new family member. Hold the baby down for the dog to see and sniff, but make sure some-one's holding the dog on lead in case of any sudden moves. Don't play keep-away or tease the dog with the baby, which only invites undesirable jump-ing up.

The dog and the baby are "family," and for starters can be treated almost as equals. Things rapidly change, however, espe-cially when baby takes to creeping around on all fours on the dog's turf or, better yet, has yummy pudding all over her face and hands! That's when a lot of things in the dog's and baby's lives become more separate than equal.

Dogs are perfect confidants.

Toddlers make terrible dog owners, but if you can't avoid the combination, use patient discipline (that is, positive teaching rather than punishment), and use time-outs before you run out of patience.

A dog and a baby (or toddler, or an assertive young child) should never be left alone together. Take the dog with you or confine him. With a baby or youngsters in the house, you'll have plenty of use for that wonderful canine safety device called a crate!

Young Children

Any dog in a house with kids will behave pretty much as the kids do, good or bad. But even good dogs and good children can get into trouble when play becomes rowdy and active.

Legs bobbing up and down, shrill voices screeching, a ball hurtling overhead, all add up to exuberant frustration for a dog who's just trying to be part of the gang. In a pack of puppies, any legs or toys being chased would be caught by a set of teeth, and all the pups involved would understand that is how the game is played. Kids do not understand this, nor do parents tolerate it. Bring Rufus indoors before you have reason to regret it. This is time-out, not a punishment.

Teach children how to play nicely with a puppy.

You can explain the situation to the children and tell them they must play quieter games until the puppy learns not to grab them with his mouth. Unfortunately, you can't explain it that easily to the dog. With adult supervision, they will learn how to play together.

Young children love to tease. Sticking their faces or wiggling their hands or fingers in the dog's face is teasing. To another person it might be just annoying, but it is threatening to a dog. There's another difference: We can make the child stop by an explanation, but the only way a dog can stop it is with a warning growl and then with teeth. Teasing is the major cause of children being bitten by their pets. Treat it seriously.

Older Children

The best age for a child to get a first dog is between the ages of 8 and 12. That's when kids are able to accept some real responsibility for their pet. Even so, take the child's vow of "I will never *ever* forget to feed (brush, walk, etc.) the dog" for what it's worth: a child's good intention at that moment. Most kids today have extra lessons, soccer practice, Little League, ballet, and so forth piled on top of school schedules. There will be many times when Mom will have to come to the dog's rescue. "I walked the dog for you so you can set the table for me" is one way to get around a missed appointment without laying on blame or guilt.

Kids in this age group make excellent obedience trainers because they are into the teaching/learning process themselves and they lack the self-consciousness of adults. Attending a dog show is something the whole family can enjoy, and watching Junior Showmanship may catch the eye of the kids. Older children can begin to get involved in many of the recreational activities that were reviewed in the previous chapter. Some of the agility obstacles, for example, can be set up in the backyard as a family project (with an adult making sure all the equipment is safe and secure for the dog).

Older kids are also beginning to look to the future, and may envision themselves as veterinarians or trainers or show dog handlers or writers of the next Lassie best-seller. Dogs are perfect confidants for these dreams. They won't tell a soul.

Other Pets

Introduce all pets tactfully. In a dog/cat situation, hold the dog, not the cat. Let two dogs meet on neutral turf—a stroll in the park or a walk down the street—with both on loose leads to permit all the normal canine ways of saying hello, including routine sniffing, circling, more sniffing, and so on. Small creatures such as hamsters, chinchillas or mice must be kept safe from their natural predators (dogs and cats).

Festive Family Occasions

Parties are great for people, but not necessarily for puppies. Until all the guests have arrived, put the dog in his crate or in a room where he won't be disturbed. A socialized dog can join the fun later as long as he's not underfoot, annoying guests or into the hors d'oeuvres.

There are a few dangers to consider, too. Doors opening and closing can allow a puppy to slip out unnoticed in the confusion, and you'll be organizing a search party instead of playing host or hostess. Party food and buffet service are not for dogs. Let Rufus party in his crate with a nice big dog biscuit.

At Christmas time, not only are tree decorations dangerous and breakable (and perhaps family heirlooms), but extreme caution should be taken with the lights, cords and outlets for the tree lights and any other festive lighting. Occasionally a dog lifts a leg, ignoring the fact that the tree is indoors. To avoid this, use a canine repellent, made for gardens, on the tree. Or keep him out of the tree room unless supervised. And whatever you do, *don't* invite trouble by hanging his toys on the tree!

Car Travel

Before you plan a vacation by car or RV with Rufus, be sure he enjoys car travel. Nothing spoils a holiday quicker than a carsick dog! Work within the dog's comfort level. Get in the car with the dog in his crate or attached to a canine car safety belt and just sit there until he relaxes. That's all. Next time, get in the car, turn on the engine and go nowhere. Just sit. When that is okay, turn on the engine and go around the block. Now you can go for a ride and include a stop where you get out, leaving the dog for a minute or two.

On a warm day, always park in the shade and leave windows open several inches. And return quickly. It only takes 10 minutes for a car to become an overheated steel death trap.

Motel or Pet Motel?

Not all motels or hotels accept pets, but you have a much better choice today than even a few years ago. To find a dog-friendly lodging, look at *On the Road Again With Man's Best Friend*, a series of directories that detail bed and breakfasts, inns, family resorts and other hotels/motels. Some places require a refundable deposit to cover any damage incurred by the dog. More B&Bs accept pets now, but some restrict the size.

If taking Rufus with you is not feasible, check out boarding kennels in your area. Your veterinarian may offer this service, or recommend a kennel or two he or she is familiar with. Go see the facilities for yourself, ask about exercise, diet, housing, and so on. Or, if you'd rather have Rufus stay home, look into bonded petsitters, many of whom will also bring in the mail and water your plants.

chapter 11

Your Dog
and your
Community

by Bardi McLennan

Step outside your home with your dog and you are no longer just family, you are both part of your community. This is when the phrase "responsible pet ownership" takes on serious implications. For starters, it means you pick up after your dog—not just occasionally, but every time your dog eliminates away from home. That means you have joined the Plastic Baggy Brigade! You always have plastic sandwich bags in your pocket and several in the car. It means you teach your kids how to use them, too. If you think this is "yucky," just imagine what the person (a non-doggy person) who inadvertently steps in the mess thinks!

Your responsibility extends to your neighbors: To their ears (no annoying barking); to their property (their garbage, their lawn, their flower beds, their cat—especially their cat); to their kids (on bikes, at play); to their kids' toys and sports equipment.

There are numerous dog-related laws, ranging from simple dog licensing and leash laws to those holding you liable for any physical injury or property damage done by your dog. These laws are in place to protect everyone in the community, including you and your dog. There are town ordinances and state laws which are by no means the same in all towns or all states. Ignorance of the law won't get you off the hook. The time to find out what the laws are where you live is now.

Be sure your dog's license is current. This is not just a good local ordinance, it can make the difference between finding your lost dog or not.

Many states now require proof of rabies vaccination and that the dog has been spayed or neutered before issuing a license. At the same time, keep up the dog's annual immunizations.

Dressing your dog up makes him appealing to strangers.

Never let your dog run loose in the neighborhood. This will not only keep you on the right side of the leash law, it's the outdoor version of the rule about not giving your dog "freedom to get into trouble."

Good Canine Citizen

Sometimes it's hard for a dog's owner to assess whether or not the dog is sufficiently socialized to be accepted by the community at large. Does Rufus or Rufina display good, controlled behavior in public? The AKC's Canine Good Citizen program is available through many dog organizations. If your dog passes the test, the title "CGC" is earned.

The overall purpose is to turn your dog into a good neighbor and to teach you about your responsibility to your community as a dog owner. Here are the ten things your dog must do willingly:

1. Accept a stranger stopping to chat with you.
2. Sit and be petted by a stranger.
3. Allow a stranger to handle him or her as a groomer or veterinarian would.
4. Walk nicely on a loose lead.
5. Walk calmly through a crowd.
6. Sit and down on command, then stay in a sit or down position while you walk away.
7. Come when called.
8. Casually greet another dog.
9. React confidently to distractions.
10. Accept being left alone with someone other than you and not become overly agitated or nervous.

Schools and Dogs

Schools are getting involved with pet ownership on an educational level. It has been proven that children who are kind to animals are humane in their attitude toward other people as adults.

A dog is a child's best friend, and so children are often primary pet owners, if not the primary caregivers. Unfortunately, they are also the ones most often bitten by dogs. This occurs due to a lack of understanding that pets, no matter how sweet, cuddly and loving, are still animals. Schools, along with parents, dog clubs, dog fanciers and the AKC, are working to change all that with video programs for children not only in grade school, but in the nursery school and pre-kindergarten age group. Teaching youngsters how to be responsible dog owners is important community work. When your dog has a CGC, volunteer to take part in an educational classroom event put on by your dog club.

Boy Scout Merit Badge

A Merit Badge for Dog Care can be earned by any Boy Scout ages 11 to 18. The requirements are not easy, but amount to a complete course in responsible dog care and general ownership. Here are just a few of the things a Scout must do to earn that badge:

> Point out ten parts of the dog using the correct names.

> Give a report (signed by parent or guardian) on your care of the dog (feeding, food used, housing, exercising, grooming and bathing), plus what has been done to keep the dog healthy.

> Explain the right way to obedience train a dog, and demonstrate three comments.

> Several of the requirements have to do with health care, including first aid, handling a hurt dog, and the dangers of home treatment for a serious ailment.

> The final requirement is to know the local laws and ordinances involving dogs.

There are similar programs for Girl Scouts and 4-H members.

Local Clubs

Local dog clubs are no longer in existence just to put on a yearly dog show. Today, they are apt to be the hub of the community's involvement with pets. Dog clubs conduct educational forums with big-name speakers, stage demonstrations of canine talent in a busy mall and take dogs of various breeds to schools for classroom discussion.

The quickest way to feel accepted as a member in a club is to volunteer your services! Offer to help with something—anything—and watch your popularity (and your interest) grow.

Therapy Dogs

Once your dog has earned that essential CGC and reliably demonstrates a steady, calm temperament, you could look into what therapy dogs are doing in your area.

Therapy dogs go with their owners to visit patients at hospitals or nursing homes, generally remaining on leash but able to coax a pat from a stiffened hand, a smile from a blank face, a few words from sealed lips or a hug from someone in need of love.

Nursing homes cover a wide range of patient care. Some specialize in care of the elderly, some in the treatment of specific illnesses, some in physical therapy. Children's facilities also welcome visits from trained therapy dogs for boosting morale in their pediatric patients. Hospice care for the terminally ill and the at-home care of AIDS patients are other areas where this canine visiting is desperately needed. Therapy dog training comes first.

Your dog can make a difference in lots of lives.

There is a lot more involved than just taking your nice friendly pooch to someone's bedside. Doing therapy dog work involves your own emotional stability as well as that of your dog. But once you have met all the requirements for this work, making the rounds once a week or once a month with your therapy dog is possibly the most rewarding of all community activities.

Disaster Aid

This community service is definitely not for everyone, partly because it is time-consuming. The initial training is rigorous, and there can be no let-up in the continuing workouts, because members are on call 24 hours a day to go wherever they are needed at a moment's notice. But if you think you would like to be able to assist in a disaster, look into search-and-rescue work. The network of search-and-rescue volunteers is worldwide, and all members of the American Rescue Dog Association (ARDA) who are qualified to do this work are volunteers who train and maintain their own dogs.

Physical Aid

Most people are familiar with Seeing Eye dogs, which serve as blind people's eyes, but not with all the other work that dogs are trained to do to assist the disabled. Dogs are also specially trained to pull wheelchairs, carry school books, pick up dropped objects, open and close doors. Some also are ears for the deaf. All these assistance-trained dogs, by the way, are allowed anywhere "No Pet" signs exist (as are therapy dogs when

Making the rounds with your therapy dog can be very rewarding.

properly identified). Getting started in any of this fascinating work requires a background in dog training and canine behavior, but there are also volunteer jobs ranging from answering the phone to cleaning out kennels to providing a foster home for a puppy. You have only to ask.

part four

Beyond
the
Basics

Recommended Reading

Books

ABOUT HEALTH CARE

Ackerman, Lowell. *Guide to Skin and Haircoat Problems in Dogs*. Loveland, Colo.: Alpine Publications, 1994.

Alderton, David. *The Dog Care Manual*. Hauppauge, N.Y.: Barron's Educational Series, Inc., 1986.

American Kennel Club. *American Kennel Club Dog Care and Training*. New York: Howell Book House, 1991.

Bamberger, Michelle, DVM. *Help! The Quick Guide to First Aid for Your Dog*. New York: Howell Book House, 1995.

Carlson, Delbert, DVM, and James Giffin, MD. *Dog Owner's Home Veterinary Handbook*. New York: Howell Book House, 1992.

DeBitetto, James, DVM, and Sarah Hodgson. *You & Your Puppy*. New York: Howell Book House, 1995.

Humphries, Jim, DVM. *Dr. Jim's Animal Clinic for Dogs*. New York: Howell Book House, 1994.

McGinnis, Terri. *The Well Dog Book*. New York: Random House, 1991.

Pitcairn, Richard and Susan. *Natural Health for Dogs*. Emmaus, Pa.: Rodale Press, 1982.

ABOUT DOG SHOWS

Hall, Lynn. *Dog Showing for Beginners*. New York: Howell Book House, 1994.

Nichols, Virginia Tuck. *How to Show Your Own Dog*. Neptune, N. J.: TFH, 1970.

Vanacore, Connie. *Dog Showing, An Owner's Guide*. New York: Howell Book House, 1990.

ABOUT TRAINING

Ammen, Amy. *Training in No Time.* New York: Howell Book House, 1995.

Baer, Ted. *Communicating With Your Dog.* Hauppauge, N.Y.: Barron's Educational Series, Inc., 1989.

Benjamin, Carol Lea. *Dog Problems.* New York: Howell Book House, 1989.

Benjamin, Carol Lea. *Dog Training for Kids.* New York: Howell Book House, 1988.

Benjamin, Carol Lea. *Mother Knows Best.* New York: Howell Book House, 1985.

Benjamin, Carol Lea. *Surviving Your Dog's Adolescence.* New York: Howell Book House, 1993.

Bohnenkamp, Gwen. *Manners for the Modern Dog.* San Francisco: Perfect Paws, 1990.

Dibra, Bashkim. *Dog Training by Bash.* New York: Dell, 1992.

Dunbar, Ian, PhD, MRCVS. *Dr. Dunbar's Good Little Dog Book,* James & Kenneth Publishers, 2140 Shattuck Ave. #2406, Berkeley, Calif. 94704. (510) 658–8588. Order from the publisher.

Dunbar, Ian, PhD, MRCVS. *How to Teach a New Dog Old Tricks,* James & Kenneth Publishers. Order from the publisher; address above.

Dunbar, Ian, PhD, MRCVS, and Gwen Bohnenkamp. Booklets on *Preventing Aggression; Housetraining; Chewing; Digging; Barking; Socialization; Fearfulness; and Fighting,* James & Kenneth Publishers. Order from the publisher; address above.

Evans, Job Michael. *People, Pooches and Problems.* New York: Howell Book House, 1991.

Kilcommons, Brian and Sarah Wilson. *Good Owners, Great Dogs.* New York: Warner Books, 1992.

McMains, Joel M. *Dog Logic—Companion Obedience.* New York: Howell Book House, 1992.

Rutherford, Clarice and David H. Neil, MRCVS. *How to Raise a Puppy You Can Live With.* Loveland, Colo.: Alpine Publications, 1982.

Volhard, Jack and Melissa Bartlett. *What All Good Dogs Should Know: The Sensible Way to Train.* New York: Howell Book House, 1991.

ABOUT BREEDING

Harris, Beth J. Finder. *Breeding a Litter, The Complete Book of Prenatal and Postnatal Care.* New York: Howell Book House, 1983.

Holst, Phyllis, DVM. *Canine Reproduction.* Loveland, Colo.: Alpine Publications, 1985.

Walkowicz, Chris and Bonnie Wilcox, DVM. *Successful Dog Breeding, The Complete Handbook of Canine Midwifery*. New York: Howell Book House, 1994.

ABOUT ACTIVITIES

American Rescue Dog Association. *Search and Rescue Dogs*. New York: Howell Book House, 1991.

Barwig, Susan and Stewart Hilliard. *Schutzhund*. New York: Howell Book House, 1991.

Beaman, Arthur S. *Lure Coursing*. New York: Howell Book House, 1994.

Daniels, Julie. *Enjoying Dog Agility—From Backyard to Competition*. New York: Doral Publishing, 1990.

Davis, Kathy Diamond. *Therapy Dogs*. New York: Howell Book House, 1992.

Gallup, Davis Anne. *Running With Man's Best Friend*. Loveland, Colo.: Alpine Publications, 1986.

Habgood, Dawn and Robert. *On the Road Again With Man's Best Friend*. New England, Mid-Atlantic, West Coast and Southeast editions. Selective guides to area bed and breakfasts, inns, hotels and resorts that welcome guests and their dogs. New York: Howell Book House, 1995.

Holland, Vergil S. *Herding Dogs*. New York: Howell Book House, 1994.

LaBelle, Charlene G. *Backpacking With Your Dog*. Loveland, Colo.: Alpine Publications, 1993.

Simmons-Moake, Jane. *Agility Training, The Fun Sport for All Dogs*. New York: Howell Book House, 1991.

Spencer, James B. *Hup! Training Flushing Spaniels the American Way*. New York: Howell Book House, 1992.

Spencer, James B. *Point! Training the All-Seasons Birddog*. New York: Howell Book House, 1995.

Tarrant, Bill. *Training the Hunting Retriever*. New York: Howell Book House, 1991.

Volhard, Jack and Wendy. *The Canine Good Citizen*. New York: Howell Book House, 1994.

General Titles

Haggerty, Captain Arthur J. *How to Get Your Pet Into Show Business*. New York: Howell Book House, 1994.

McLennan, Bardi. *Dogs and Kids, Parenting Tips*. New York: Howell Book House, 1993.

Moran, Patti J. *Pet Sitting for Profit, A Complete Manual for Professional Success*. New York: Howell Book House, 1992.

Scalisi, Danny and Libby Moses. *When Rover Just Won't Do, Over 2,000 Suggestions for Naming Your Dog.* New York: Howell Book House, 1993.

Sife, Wallace, PhD. *The Loss of a Pet.* New York: Howell Book House, 1993.

Wrede, Barbara J. *Civilizing Your Puppy.* Hauppauge, N.Y.: Barron's Educational Series, 1992.

Magazines

The AKC GAZETTE, The Official Journal for the Sport of Purebred Dogs. American Kennel Club, 51 Madison Ave., New York, NY.

Bloodlines Journal. United Kennel Club, 100 E. Kilgore Rd., Kalamazoo, MI.

Dog Fancy. Fancy Publications, 3 Burroughs, Irvine, CA 92718

Dog World. Maclean Hunter Publishing Corp., 29 N. Wacker Dr., Chicago, IL 60606.

Videos

"SIRIUS Puppy Training," by Ian Dunbar, PhD, MRCVS. James & Kenneth Publishers, 2140 Shattuck Ave. #2406, Berkeley, CA 94704. Order from the publisher.

"Training the Companion Dog," from Dr. Dunbar's British TV Series, James & Kenneth Publishers. (See address above).

The American Kennel Club produces videos on every breed of dog, as well as on hunting tests, field trials and other areas of interest to purebred dog owners. For more information, write to AKC/Video Fulfillment, 5580 Centerview Dr., Suite 200, Raleigh, NC 27606.

13

Resources

Breed Clubs

Every breed recognized by the American Kennel Club has a national (parent) club. National clubs are a great source of information on your breed. You can get the name of the secretary of the club by contacting:

The American Kennel Club
51 Madison Avenue
New York, NY 10010
(212) 696-8200

There are also numerous all-breed, individual breed, obedience, hunting and other special-interest dog clubs across the country. The American Kennel Club can provide you with a geographical list of clubs to find ones in your area. Contact them at the above address.

Registry Organizations

Registry organizations register purebred dogs. The American Kennel Club is the oldest and largest in this country, and currently recognizes over 130 breeds. The United Kennel Club registers some breeds the AKC doesn't (including the American Pit Bull Terrier and the Miniature Fox Terrier) as well as many of the same breeds. The others included here are for your reference; the AKC can provide you with a list of foreign registries.

155

American Kennel Club
51 Madison Avenue
New York, NY 10010

United Kennel Club (UKC)
100 E. Kilgore Road
Kalamazoo, MI 49001-5598

American Dog Breeders Assn.
P.O. Box 1771
Salt Lake City, UT 84110
(Registers American Pit Bull Terriers)

Canadian Kennel Club
89 Skyway Avenue
Etobicoke, Ontario
Canada M9W 6R4

National Stock Dog Registry
P.O. Box 402
Butler, IN 46721
(Registers working stock dogs)

Orthopedic Foundation for Animals (OFA)
2300 E. Nifong Blvd.
Columbia, MO 65201-3856
(Hip registry)

Activity Clubs

Write to these organizations for information on the
activities they sponsor.

American Kennel Club
51 Madison Avenue
New York, NY 10010
(Conformation Shows, Obedience Trials, Field
Trials and Hunting Tests, Agility, Canine Good

Citizen, Lure Coursing, Herding, Tracking,
Earthdog Tests, Coonhunting.)

United Kennel Club
100 E. Kilgore Road
Kalamazoo, MI 49001-5598
(Conformation Shows, Obedience Trials, Agility,
Hunting for Various Breeds, Terrier Trials and
more.)

North American Flyball Assn.
1342 Jeff St.
Ypsilanti, MI 48198

International Sled Dog Racing Assn.
P.O. Box 446
Norman, ID 83848-0446

North American Working Dog Assn., Inc.
Southeast Kreisgruppe
P.O. Box 833
Brunswick, GA 31521

Trainers

Association of Pet Dog Trainers
P.O. Box 3734
Salinas, CA 93912
(408) 663–9257

American Dog Trainers' Network
161 West 4th St.
New York, NY 10014
(212) 727–7257

**National Association of Dog Obedience
Instructors**
2286 East Steel Rd.
St. Johns, MI 48879

Beyond the
Basics

Associations

American Dog Owners Assn.
1654 Columbia Tpk.
Castleton, NY 12033
(Combats anti-dog legislation)

Delta Society
P.O. Box 1080
Renton, WA 98057-1080
(Promotes the human/animal bond through
pet-assisted therapy and other programs)

Dog Writers Assn. of America (DWAA)
Sally Cooper, Secy.
222 Woodchuck Ln.
Harwinton, CT 06791

National Assn. for Search and Rescue (NASAR)
P.O. Box 3709
Fairfax, VA 22038

Therapy Dogs International
6 Hilltop Road
Mendham, NJ 07945

2